A CONVERSATION
WITH AN ANGEL

A CONVERSATION
WITH AN ANGEL

·AND·OTHER·ESSAYS·BY·

Hilaire Belloc

Essay Index Reprint Series

 BOOKS FOR LIBRARIES PRESS
FREEPORT, NEW YORK

LIBRARY OF CONGRESS CATALOG CARD NUMBER:
68-16907
PRINTED IN THE UNITED STATES OF AMERICA

DEDICATED
TO
ELIZABETH HERBERT

The greater part of these papers appeared in the 'New Statesman' and the 'Saturday Review,' to the Editors of which my thanks are due.

CONTENTS

CONTENTS

A CONVERSATION
WITH AN ANGEL

A Conversation with an Angel

THE OTHER DAY I FOUND MYSELF IN A PRO-
VINCIAL TOWN ABROAD WHERE THERE WAS A
large cathedral church. On the south side of the
south-western door of this church there was an
Angel quite fifteen feet high. He was carved in
stone and looked as though he were younger than
King John of England, but older than St. Louis of
France. He had bobbed hair and a pleasing but
exceedingly intriguing smile, and he wore a fringe.
In his hand he held pressed up against his chest
('stomach' I would have said, were it not for the
respect I owe him) a large round dial, which was
a sundial; and the rusted gnomon was still there,
marking the hours.

As I stood looking at him he asked me whether
I could suggest a motto for his sundial, for it
had none.

I said, 'It seems to me a very silly thing to have
given you a sundial without a motto; since it is

proper to sundials to have mottoes—sometimes good, sometimes bad—usually bad.'

He said that he agreed with me, but that the reason no motto had been put upon *this* sundial was that the man who had made it could not write, and that was why he was such a good artist. 'For,' said the Angel, 'you must admit that I am extraordinarily well made.'

I agreed with him, but said that it was no cause for self-gratulation, but rather for congratulating the artist. To this the Angel assented, but not very graciously. I would have gone on to draw a moral from this and have explained to the Angel never to be proud of any talent whatever, let alone of the mere body, even if it were fifteen feet high and of stone, because such things are gifts. The only things which we can fully call our own are our vices, and even of this (I told him) scientific men are now in some doubt. But he cut me short by asking me again whether I had a motto for him.

I thought a little while and then said to him, 'I can only give you a motto in English.' Our conversation up to this had been conducted in a simple kind of chronicle Latin and in early French: the *Langue d'Oil.* He said that all languages were the same to him, and that he understood them all. I

did not believe this. But I gave him his motto,
which I wrote out on a postcard so as to remember it:

In sweet deluding lies let fools delight.
A shadow marks our days, which end in night.

The Angel said it was very pretty—very nice indeed.

He then said, after a pause, that because I had a
sort of pronunciation different from what he was
used to he had not quite caught my meaning. I
translated it for him into the Language of Oil,
whereat he was somewhat taken aback and said,
'I certainly could not have a motto like that! It is
un-Christian! You must give me another.'

So I gave him:

Suns may set and suns may rise,
Our poor eyes
When their little light is past
Droop and go to sleep at last.

With this, the Angel said he would have nothing
to do. He said it was simply a bad imitation of
Catullus and that he met Catullus too often to run
the risk of bad translations of him on his dial.

I asked him how he could meet Catullus, seeing
he was stuck up on a wall and had not been able
to move for all these centuries and centuries. He
said it was the eternal part of him that met Catullus,

3

and I said that I could make neither head nor tail of what he was talking about; whereat he began a long discourse upon images and their habiting spirits, their dual function, the limits of the veneration that should be paid to them, and I don't know what and all. But I interrupted him by asking why he had not noticed the real disadvantage of the motto, which was, that it did not apply to sundials, and that caused him to ask me to try again.

I thought a little while about it as is my custom when I compose immortal verse, and produced this:

How slow the shadow creeps, but when 'tis passed,
How fast the shadows fall: How fast! How fast!

'What was that?' said the Angel.

'That was my third motto,' said I proudly.

'I don't like it,' said the Angel. 'In the first place it is not true. In this climate it is well known that night comes very slowly; there is a prolonged twilight. I watch it out of the corner of my right eye every fine evening. You ought to thank Heaven that you are of the North. To talk about the night "ruining down" is to talk like a nigger.'

'I never did say that night "ruined down,"' I answered. 'I wouldn't dream of using such Drury Lane language.'

4

'No, but your sort do,' reiterated the Angel, 'and that was the kind of thing you had in mind.'

'Nor does it matter whether the thing is true or not, the point is the poetry,' I retorted.

'Not in mottoes,' said the Angel. 'In mottoes the point *is* the truth, as the butter-merchant said when he bought a peerage and took the motto, *"Dieu seul."* '

'Well,' said I, 'if you don't like my motto you can leave it. I am sorry you should do so because it is a very good motto. I know that it is good because I feel at the back of my mind that I copied it from somewhere. Verses that are traditional and copied from somewhere unconsciously are always better than your original, sudden, uncooked stuff. But if you don't like it, why, as I say, you can leave it.'

'I will,' said the Angel.

'Shall I make you yet another?' I asked, being now filled with vanity in spite of my rebuffs, and also warming to my work as poets will after the first half-hour.

'If you like,' said the Angel without enthusiasm.

So I again thought for some time, remaining silent and attempting to compose. At last he could bear it no longer and said, 'Hurry up.' I told him that it was hopeless. I had no more mottoes for sundials. In fact, he might have seen for himself that I was petering out, by the way in which the middle one had not fitted in. 'Then,' he said, 'if you have no more mottoes for sundials I have no more use for you, and I shall not say another word,' nor did he.

I still addressed him, with irony, with solicitude, with insult, with affection, with command: in all the seven moods which inflect the Basque vocative. But he remained dumb, nobly illustrating the sentiment of the psalm *In Exitu*, wherein it is thundered out that images of stone have mouths, but cannot speak and cannot clamour in their gutturals.

I gave it up as a bad job, and left him for the night so that he might have time to recover his temper; but when I went back the next morning before taking my train, to see whether he was in a more genial mood, he still remained offensively and pig-headedly silent, carrying his ironical smile in a fixed, exasperating manner, which showed me that he knew all about the great world. So I left him to it, and was gone.

I have asked friends who have been in the place since. Some say they have spoken with him, others say they have not. I believe those who say they have not, partly because it makes me proud to think I was the only man with whom he exchanged words during all that long space of seven centuries, and partly because, though I know, of course, that statues certainly *can* speak, and do so on occasion, yet those occasions are exceedingly rare.

That conversation with an Angel was held nearly a month ago, and during all that while I have not been able to make up any more mottoes for sundials.

II

On Turbots and Sea-Horses

WE LIVE IN A TIME WHICH DOES NOT ALLOW THE LEAST SUSPICION OF HERESY. EVERYONE has to be orthodox, under pain of being gagged—which is, after all, a more efficacious way of suppressing heresy than the mere suppression of the heretic. I will not, therefore, in what I am about to say, suggest any false doctrine; I only propose to ask a few questions connected with my going to the new Aquarium of the Zoological Gardens in London.

I could say a great many things about that Aquarium which would be perfectly orthodox, and on which there could be no question of gagging. For instance, I could say that it is very well organised; that the lighting of the water is very effective; that it is very clean; that it is the best thing of its kind in Europe—and so on. In all these I should have the hearty support of my contemporaries, because it would give them a vague feeling that they are fine fellows and the superiors of the rest of the world.

Now for the difficulties. I watched those entertaining—and I am afraid rather stupid—creatures, the fishes, for an afternoon. I was absorbed in them. And the more I watched them the more doubt arose in my wretchedly unorthodox mind.

To begin with, the Turbot. I came to a tank where a Turbot was lying on some rather mottled sand. It was white sand with greyish patches, some of the patches a little darker than others. The Turbot lay upon the sand, flat. It was quite impossible to distinguish which was sand and which was Turbot! The back of the Turbot was not *like* the sand; it was *identical* with the sand. At an inch off you could not tell sand from Turbot. I have never seen anything like it! I have seen insects that look like twigs, and moths or butterflies (I forget which) which look like dead leaves, and pompous men at dinner who, so long as they do not talk, look like statues carved in lard. But I have never seen a living organism actually identical in appearance with dead matter—until I saw this Turbot.

Now I put this question to you—I suggest, as the lawyers say, this question: how did it come about? If you tell me that it came about through Turbots having got a little more like the mottled sand through countless generations by a process of natural selection, that answer at once suggests to me about fifteen hundred more questions, of which, for the love I bear you, I will spare you the greater part; but at least consider these.

Why only the Turbot? Why not the Great Kissing Conger Eel? Why not the Yawning Salamander, who in the very next tank was lying as black as your hat upon the white sand? Why not any one of these innumerable creatures? Why only the Turbot?

And, again, if he took shots like this, or rather, if he did not take shots, but blindly arrived at such an end by a process of infinitely small differentiations in which more sand-like Turbots survived than less sand-like, why was he exactly like that particular bit of sand? There are many kinds of sand in the sea, and many sorts of earths and gravel on the sea-floor, of all sorts and colours Why did he choose just that particular bit of sand? And, again, if that is the way he got his amazing top side, what are the stages by which he got there? How is it he has reached the goal, and nothing around him is on its way to a similar goal?

You will admit that there are a good many questions to be asked, and for my part I cannot see the answer to them.

A little farther on I saw for the first time a small animal called the Sea-Horse. It was astonishingly like a horse, and what was much more astonishing it was astonishingly like the pictures which I had seen of it in the books of my boyhood. Therein was I surprised; for things in reality are almost always different from the pictures one has seen of them. I know by experience how unlike are the Bay of Naples and St. Mark's of Venice from the pictures I have seen of them. But the Sea-Horse came up to sample, except that he was much smaller than I thought he would be. He was about the size of my thumb.

Now, how did he come to be so like a horse? If it were chance, then there ought to be any number of forms more or less like horses, and only he exactly like a horse. If it be not chance, what is it?

In many ways he is unlike a horse. He is not nearly so big; he does not eat hay; he is not (to all appearance) nervous; and he lives under water. It is one in any countless number of powers of a million; one chance in what you may call infinity, that a little creature under the sea should have the profile of a horse. How did he come to get it?

Then I found another little fish, which was, for the most part, just like any other little fish—oblong and with a tail, with a vacant expression and too large a mouth, very flabby and something peevish, but differing from all other fishes in this, that he had an exceedingly bright, definite, hard half-circle of violent red over each eye. It looked like coral. Now, how did he get that? The orthodox answer is that he got it because it helped him to survive. I do not see that it could have done that, nor (if it did) why it should be of that particular shape and extreme definition and oddity, and so different from the rest of him.

I propose, to all such questions, an answer, which I only set down in fear and trembling, because I know the penalty attaching to this rebellion against the orthodox doctrine of my time and place. I think the answer is that we do not know. Indeed, I have read a magnificent work of Vailleton on Morphology (though that was on vertebrates). It has roared through the old Darwinian dogmas like a nine-inch shell; Vailleton of Montpellier; and at the very end of that great work this is the very thought he expresses, in substance as follows:

'How did all this come about? Certainly not as the orthodox science of twenty or thirty years ago insisted. That I have proved. Then how (you will ask me) did it come about? I do not know.'

III

On Poverty

I HAD OCCASION THE OTHER DAY TO GIVE AN
ADDRESS TO A NUMBER OF YOUNG MEN UPON
the matter of Poverty: which address I had intended
to call 'Poverty: The Attainment of It: the Reten-
tion of It when Attained.' But I found that no ex-
planation of my title was necessary. The young men
knew all about it.

In giving this short address I discovered, as one
always does in the course of speaking without notes,
all manner of new aspects in the thing. The simple
straightforward view of poverty we all know; how
it is beneficial to the soul, what a training it is, how
acceptable to the Higher Powers, and so on. We
also know how all those men whom we are taught to
admire began with poverty, and we all have, I hope,
at the back of our minds a conception of poverty as
a sort of foundation for virtue and right living.

But these ideas are general and vague. I was
led by my discourse to consider the thing in detail,

13

and to think out by reminiscence and reason certain small, solid, particular advantages in poverty, and also a sort of theory of maintenance in poverty: rules for remaining poor.

I thus discovered first of all a definition of poverty, which is this: Poverty is that state in which a man is perpetually anxious for the future of himself and his dependents, unable to pursue life upon a standard to which he was brought up, tempted both to subservience and to a sour revolt, and tending inexorably towards despair.

Such was the definition of poverty at which I arrived, and once arrived at, the good effects flowing from such a condition are very plain.

The first great good attendant upon poverty is that it makes men generous. You will notice that while some few of the rich are avaricious or mean, and while all of them have to be, from the very nature of their position, careful, the poor and embarrassed man will easily share whatever little he has. True, this is from no good motive, but merely from a conviction that, whatever he does, it will be much the same in the end; so that his kindness to his fellows comes from a mixture of weakness and indifference. Still, it breeds a habit; and that is why men whose whole characters have been formed under this kind of poverty always throw away money when by any chance they get a lump of it.

Then there is this other good attending poverty, that it cures one of illusions. The most irritating thing in the company of the rich, and especially of rich women, is the very morass of illusion in which they live. Indeed, it cannot be all illusion, there must be a good deal of conscious falsehood about it. But, at any rate, it is an abyss of unreality, communion with which at last becomes intolerable. Now the poor man is physically prevented from falling into such vices of the heart and intelligence. He cannot possibly think that the police are heroes, the judges superhuman beings, the motives of public men in general other than vile. He can nourish no fantasies upon the kind old family servant, or the captain of industry's supreme intelligence. The poor man is up against it, as the phrase goes. He is up against the bullying and corruption of the police, the inhuman stupidity of the captain of industry, the sly self-advancement of the lawyer, the abominable hypocrisies of the parasitical trades: such as buttling. He comes across all these things by contact and the direct personal sensible experience. He can no more think of mankind as a garden than a soldier can

15

think of war as a picture, or a sailor of the sea as a pleasure-place.

We may also thank poverty (those of us who are enjoying her favours) for cutting quite out of our lives certain extraordinary necessities which haunt our richer brethren. I know a rich man who is under compulsion to change his clothes at least twice a day, and often thrice, to travel at set periods to set places, and to see in rotation each of at least sixty people. He has less freedom than a schoolboy in school, or a corporal in a regiment; indeed, he has no real leisure at all, because so many things are thus necessary to him. But your poor man cannot even conceive what these necessities may be. If you were to tell him that he *had* to go and soak himself in the vulgarity of the Riviera for so many weeks, he would not understand the word 'had' at all. He would say that perhaps there were some people who liked that kind of thing, but that anyone should do it without a strongly perverted appetite he could not understand.

And here's another boon of grinding, anxious, sordid poverty. There is no greater enemy of the soul than sloth; but in this state of ceaseless dull exasperation, like a kind of grumbling toothache, sloth is impossible. Yet another enemy of the soul is pride, and even the sour poor man cannot really nourish pride; he may wish to nourish it; he may hope in future to nourish it; but he cannot immediately nourish it. Or, again, the inmost of man which an old superstition called 'the Soul' is hurt by luxury. Now poverty, in the long run, forbids or restricts luxury.

I know very well you will tell me with countless instances how the poor gentlemen of your acquaintance drink cocktails, eat caviare, go to the theatre (and that in the stalls), take taxis, order liqueurs with their coffee and blow cheques. Very true, but if you will narrowly watch the careers of such, you will find that there is a progressive decline in these habits of theirs. The taxis get rarer and rarer after forty-five; caviare dies out; and though liqueur with coffee goes on, there is discipline, incredible as it may seem, imposed upon luxury by poverty. Indeed, I met a man only last April in a town called Lillebonne (where I was examining the effects of Roman remains upon hotel-keeping), and this man told me that before the War he habitually spent his holiday (he was a parson) in Switzerland, but now he could not get beyond Normandy. Whereupon I sketched for him on a piece of paper a scheme showing, with a radius vector (the same graduated, which, indeed, was my parson, also) and drawn to scale, the expenses of a holiday. Therein did I show him that a holiday killing lions in East Africa cost so much, another badgering the French in Morocco so much, another annoying the Spaniards so much: and how the cheapest holiday of all was a holiday on foot in Normandy, which lies but one poor Bradbury from the coasts of these islands. This little diagram he folded and took away—little knowing that a still cheaper holiday could be taken in the Ardennes.

Poverty, I think, however, has a much nobler effect by the introduction of irony, which I take to be the salt in the feast of intelligence. I have, indeed, known rich men to possess irony native to themselves, so that it is like a picture which a man paints for his own pleasure and puts up on his own walls. All the poor of London have irony, and, indeed, poor men all over the world have irony; even poor gentlemen, after the age of fifty, discover veins of irony and are the better for them, as a man is better for sherry in his soup. Remark that irony kills stupid satire, and that to have an agent within one that kills stupid satire is to possess an antiseptic against the suppurative reactions of the mind.

Poverty, again, makes men appreciate reality. You may tell me that this is of no advantage. It is of no direct advantage, but I am sure it is of advantage in the long run, for if you ignore reality you will come sooner or later against it, like a ship against a rock in a fog, and you will suffer as the ship will suffer.

If you say to the rich man that some colleague of his has genius, he may admit it in a lazy but sincere fashion. A poor man knows better; he may admit it with his lips, but he is not so foolish as to accept it.

Lastly, of poverty, I think this, that it prepares one very carefully for the grave. I heard it said once by a beggar in a passion that the rich took nothing with them down to death. In the literal acceptation of the text he was wrong, for the rich take down with them to death flattery, folly, illusion, pride and a good many lesser garments which have grown into their skins, and the tearing off of which at the great stripping must hurt a good deal. But I know what this mendicant meant—he meant that they take nothing with them down to the grave in the way of motor-cars, hot water, clean change of clothes, and various intolerably boring games. The rich go down to death stripped of external things not grown into their skins; the poor go down to death stripped of everything. Therefore in Charon's boat they get forward, and are the first upon the further shore. And this, I suppose, is some sort of advantage.

IV

On Getting Rid of People

I DIVIDE THE WORLD, AFTER A LONG, WIDE-SPREAD, AND DETAILED EXPERIENCE OF THE beastly place—and when I say 'the world,' I mean I divide the people of the world—into three groups, of very different sizes—the people who can get rid of other people smoothly and without offence; the people who can do it with a certain amount of normal friction; and the people who can only do it at the expense of heavy trouble, during which they are grossly insulted or subjected to intolerable humiliation.

The middle group is immensely the largest; it covers the great mass of the human race (poor coves!).

They get rid of people as they do everything else; jogging along more or less, no extreme either way, finding life hard yet bearable; liking moderately; disliking very little; more moved than moving. Such is the lump, such is the general paste or dough out of which humanity is—not sufficiently—baked. You may see your Cabinet Minister, your Racing Tout, your Innkeeper, your Lord, your Publisher, breaking off with a bore and leaving both himself and the bore a little ruffled—but not too much. Now and then this common man, this general type, will find the process a little more difficult than usual, just as sometimes a plaster will stick a little harder than usual. The fellow-being can only be dismissed with some effort, and in consequence there is a rowlet, or rowkin, a diminutive row; nothing severe, but enough to cause at most a day's annoyance.

But do not be Nominalist. Do not tell me that here (or in any other matter) there are no real categories, no distinct ideas. This middle type of men, this average of getting rid of others, ends sharply either way. There is a gulf between him and his two fellows—the one above who can always get rid of other people to their joy, and the one below who cannot do it without monstrous conflict and peril and sharp pain.

As for these last, they are not many, but they have among them the most noble and therefore the most unfortunate. Every good poet I have known —and I have known two—was of this kind; recluses are of this kind, and the greater part of saints; not a few scholars, and every one without exception of that rare sort which, without a word and often without a gesture, impresses Truth upon others.

All these in getting rid of others are in for heavy weather. They cannot do it without some violent scene or at the best a permanent enmity—and yet they have to do it all day long, for they are just the sort whom the rest of the world is perpetually harrying—with lassoes, snares, traps, nets, gins, and sticky lime, to catch them with, whether as lions or as supports for those who need support, or as creators for those who hunger to hear good verse, fixed wisdom or even holiness. These are just the men who have to go through all their lives shaking off other people, and not a day of that life passes without ensuing trouble through their inability to be rid of their kind with smoothness.

That is why you find them sometimes darting down side streets, shouting 'not at home' out of a window at the upturned face, or scribbling notes in which they lie about their movements, or sinking (alas!) to the baseness of getting letters posted from distant towns that they may simulate absence. With this great faculty for suffering in the getting rid of others goes the faculty of losing money, of making bad bargains, of being done in the eye, and in general all the bitterness of the Sucker's life.

Of you who are reading this, too many, feeling moved by my description of the man thus burdened, will make sure you belong to that little company of the martyred heroes. You flatter yourselves. They are but a very little band; and if they bear the mark of suffering, it is because such a badge is the stamp of the elect.

What, then, shall I say of that other band, at the remote end of the spectrum, the people who can get rid of others smoothly and in a mutual air of beatitude? Oh! Those are the fortunate of this world! I do not envy them their eternal fate —but their fate between the registrar and the registrar, their fate between the nursery and the nursing home, is the fate of the fortunate few, of the rare minority, of the Men who make Good.

How often have I watched them at it!

I do not count women, for all women have the trick. I am talking only of my own sex. Most of the men who have accumulated great fortunes at the expense of their fellows have this faculty. They are gone, and you hardly know that they are gone; or they have dismissed you, and you leave them under the belief that they were reluctant to lose you, but you had to tear yourself away. It is as though a friendly hand were being put upon your shoulder (the other hand is often in your pocket) and you were being begged to stay, when in truth you were being kicked out.

For the fortunate clique of glad-ridders carry with them a natural protective colouring, a natural atmosphere of deceit, granted them by their natural Lord of the Unseen World Below. We do not recognise them. At least, only those of us (and I am one) who meditate at length upon the actions of their fellows can pick this species out from among the millions of mankind. I have heard it said that the art can be acquired. I doubt it. For I have watched men who by birth and training should have possessed it, men in great position, compelled by that position to grin at humanity all day long, and to carry the 'What can I do for you?' rictus through all the years of manhood, and not one in a hundred has the strange gift. Mark how other men talk of the man of position: their resentment against him, their stories of his rudeness, of his blundering—it is always a reminiscence of having been got rid of.

Here and there a man of position has the occult power. I knew one myself, the son of a small blackmailer. He had fine presence, great fortune and high office in the State, and could have got rid of Lord Chesterfield himself with success. But he owed his rare gift to nature, not to his peerage.

Some of the fortunate of whom I speak have the gift in so high a degree that even experienced people like myself are deceived; and I remember one in particular whom I only found out by over-hearing him on the telephone. All that he said to me upon the telephone was gracious and good, and like a spring wood to the nostrils of my soul. But his wife, or some such person, happened to be standing by him, and not appreciating the sensitiveness of the magical instrument, he addressed her in asides.

Thus he would alternate:

(*To me*): 'Ah, that *will* be good! Then at three o'clock, then?—eh?'

(*To his wife, or what not*): 'Goodness gracious, my dear, it isn't *my* fault! *I* can't make him stop!'

(*To me*): 'Wednesday? Excellent! . . . Don't go away. I have such a lot of things to say to you!'

(*To the what not*): 'I'm *coming*, my dear, I tell you I'm *coming*. He's bound to stop soon. He can't go on talking all day.'

(*To me*): 'I say! You haven't sent me your book. Oh! Damn! They've cut me off, I can't hear any-thing!'

26

(*To the what not*): 'That's stopped him, I think!'

By such a revelation did I penetrate into the black heart of this one, whom I will call Fortunatus; and from that day I have hated him. He is dead these fifteen years, and I hate him still. But, then, it is human and right to hate the fortunate.

On Academic Hate

ALL THINGS ARE FUNNY WHICH ARE OUT OF PROPORTION, AND THERE IS ONE PARTICU-larly funny thing, the funniness of which depends upon a monstrous disproportion; that funny thing has no regular name. Some of my friends call it the Ille Sceleratissimus Brunckius. It is the monstrous rage of the learned. It is the modern form of the old odium theologicum.

I know all about it, for I have had it myself, and I have lived for years in places where it flourished exceedingly. It is inexhaustibly comic.

A man has read all there is to read about a particular campaign; let us say, all the exceedingly unsatisfactory short and scrappy evidence on Hannibal's crossing of the Alps. He has read all round his subject as well, and he has visited the place and studied the ground. He comes to a conclusion; for instance, that Hannibal crossed by the Little St. Bernard.

Another man comes along who has done just the same thing—read all the very short and exceedingly unsatisfactory evidence, read all round the subject and concludes that Hannibal crossed by the Great St. Bernard. It does not in the least matter where he crossed. It is one of those very few controversial things in history which are not connected with any more-or-less-conscious religious motive. It is a thing which you can go on debating for ever, because the evidence is insufficient, and because you do not know whether your witnesses are telling the truth or amusing themselves.

The sparring begins. At first the antagonists are reasonably polite. I notice that they even compliment each other in public, through a subtle form of pride; for each in so doing gives the audience to understand that he and his opponent belong to a very special and important and small group of superior beings. Letters and articles are exchanged.

Then, somewhere about the third or fourth letter or controversial article, fermentation begins, and with it the fun. One of them accuses the other of lying, or ignorance, or both. The other answers by marvelling how any human being could be so stupid as to have misunderstood his simple phrase, or so bestially blind to the texts. In a little while they are hurling insults at each other as violently as if each had murdered the other's child. Then there comes the stage when the anger is speechless, 'too full for sound or foam.'

The average honest man coming across controversies of this kind is bewildered; the very good man is saddened. As for me, I am enormously amused.

Whenever I hear that one of these little scraps has arisen, I make eagerly for the papers, where I can read the mutual abuse of the combatants, and I always feel a disappointment as I see the stage of exhaustion or speechlessness approaching.

It is especially funny when the two men are really learned upon a very obscure point of which I, the reader, know nothing whatever. There were two men at it some years ago upon a Lithuanian word, and I am as innocent of Lithuanian as it is possible for a man to be. They brought out whole regiments of funny-looking words, spelt diabolically, and they would appeal in the most *naïve* manner to the attendant human race, asking whether the conclusion were not clear—though not one man out of ten thousand who read them had the least idea what it was all about.

Then I remember another case, upon a subject which I had read up rather carefully, to wit, the fate of the house which Robespierre once inhabited in the Rue St.-Honoré. How much of it, if any of it, remained?

This controversy was carried on between two men, each writing in a review dealing with the French Revolution alone. Each, by the way, was representative of the two divisions into which the great French religious and political quarrel falls; but there could be no conceivable reason why the Republican Atheist should have wanted Robespierre's house to remain (or to have disappeared—I forget which it was), or why the Royalist Christian should have wished it to disappear (or remain). All I know is, that long before the dozen articles were polished off, one was accusing the other of being a forger, and the other was accusing the first of deliberate lying.

It was great fun. I felt myself so strongly thirty years ago on the subject of the three-field system of agriculture and its survival from Roman times, that for several months I could not trust myself to meet an honest gentleman who knew more about it than I, and was probably as wrong as I was. And I have known a case of two life-long friends, belonging to the same club, who became (and have remained) irreconcilable enemies, over the question of a London street, whether it did or did not, two hundred years ago, end in a blind alley.

The material for these quarrels always has the same character. In the first place there must be no possibility for victory; that is, there must be no evidence that is overwhelming, so convincing to every plain man that the man quoting it is unanswerable. No, the essential of this huge joke, which we are happily permitted to enjoy, is a vague and doubtful hypothesis. Thus, in that matter of Hannibal's circus, you have to guess what 'four days' distance from' may mean, whether four days' marching or posting. Having discovered that, you have to guess from what point the distance was taken. Then you have the pleasing feature of a piece of land called 'an island'—of course it is not an island. It is either the land between the Durance and the Isere, or between the Isere and the Rhone. You have to identify a white rock (in the Alps, ye gods! in all the Alps, one white rock between Lake Leman and the Mediterranean!). Then you have to find a place on a pass from which you can see the plains of Italy below you, supposing always that the speech mentioning them was really made—of which there is no certitude whatever. Supposing Hannibal did make that speech, you must decide whether it were not empty rhetoric—for a man can point to the plains of Italy without seeing them, just as the accused politician will point proudly to the honour of his public career, although it is not there. Anyhow, there would be no controversy about Hannibal's march, and there would be no friendships broken over it, and we should not, any of us, have the amusement of watching vigorous blows delivered and horrible insults hurled in that connection, if we had full evidence of what happened. The first essential of this farce is vague hypothesis.

The second essential is learning. No superficial man falls into those grotesque rages. It is only the men who really have gone right into the subject who are seized by the madness.

Now, whence does this madness proceed? What are the rights of the thing? I have never been able to analyse it. I have never understood it. I only know that this mood arises and is utterly irrational. That a man should hate another to death over some loved object would be comprehensible; but no one can love a dry theory. That a man should resent insult is natural; but the exchange of insults in these quarrels is an effect and not a cause.

Hackneyed as the theme is, I have an original contribution to make. There is no one of us but, upon the arising of one of these quarrels (and you get them in the learned world every week), can do the thing that is at once most amusing and worthy; there is no one of us but can play the part of peacemaker towards the end of the quarrel, and at the same time vastly increase its comedy. I will tell you how this is done.

Just before the antagonists get to the speechless stage, barge in with some grossly ignorant suggestion; the sort of thing which you might get out of a popular Universal History of the World. It is wise to do this under an assumed name. For instance, when they are at shrieking point over Hannibal's passage of the Alps, suggest a third pass, and give some asinine reason for it. When one man is out for the Mont Genèvre and the other for the Little St. Bernard, take the Mont Cenis, and make it start from the wrong valley, saying at the same time that the Mont Cenis was open when the others were already blocked, and that you can see the plains of Italy quite clearly from it if you leave the road and climb up one of the foothills. Then the two boxing men will forget their quarrel in order to throw off their gloves, and turn upon you and rend you with their views. It is no bad fun, after having led them on a little, to admit you know noth-

34

ing about it, and that you were only joining in the game because it seemed so exciting.

I did that once, years ago, in the matter of an archæological discussion in my own country, and I laugh over the memory of it yet.

VI

Dickens Revisited

I HAVE LATELY RETURNED TO MY DICKENS AFTER A VERY GREAT MANY YEARS. NOT THAT I WOULD not in the interval have read him, but that fatigue hampered me, and the sheer necessity for getting away from letters altogether. Lately I have had an opportunity to return, and I have begun with two books, *Dombey and Son* and *Nicholas Nickleby*. The first I had not opened, to my certain knowledge, since the year 1897; the second I had not opened, I think, since the year 1901. I propose very humbly to set down what effect they make upon me in the year 1926. Not that I pretend to any critical power, but that I would like to establish a brief personal record showing what one person of my generation feels about this writer upon so mature a return to his work. I have no critical faculty; I know very well that the emotions he arouses in me will differ from those which they arouse in most of my readers. And I don't pretend that these emotions are rightly

36

aroused in me. On the contrary, it is exceedingly likely that I am wrong, not in my judgment, for I cannot call it judgment, but in what is called to-day my 'reaction.'

I was at first puzzled, and am still interested to consider, wherein the greatness of the writer lies. The first thing a modern like myself would say about him is that he is damnably crude, with black and white contrasting like a silhouette show; that there are only two values in his pictures and that these two are simply and violently thrown up, one against the other, as they are in a popular poster. But, then, that is true of Molière, and on the whole, with some few exceptions, it is true of Shakespeare's characters, though Shakespeare is much more interested in complexity, of course, than Dickens was. I take it, therefore, that this crudity is no bar to greatness in writing. When Richard III comes on to the stage and snarls with surprising candour that he is a vile fellow, and tells you all about it, it is quite out of nature, but it is a good piece of writing all the same. This crudity in Dickens, however, seems to me to go a little beyond the line, when you analyse it in one particular, which is, that he produces a character by a single trick, wherein he is, as in everything else, essentially an actor of melodrama. Each of his characters has one tag, and exists by the repetition of that tag, and by no other. All his plots turn on one and only one note. Yet in spite of such insufficiency the character and machinery of all or nearly all his figures have intense life, and his stories a most powerful interest: and that is a very remarkable thing. So that I can only say, as one can only say of one hundred other successes in the art of letters: 'How it is done, I know not, but it is done.'

Another thing which has struck me in this return to Dickens, is the amazing power of his good rhetoric in the midst of whole washtubs of bad rhetoric. Of the badness of his bad rhetoric I suppose no competent judge will doubt, or, if any man does doubt it, why, then, he doubts it. I do not, and more I cannot say. I am as certain that the mass of Dickens's rhetoric, especially his sentimental rhetoric, is bad writing, as I am that the architecture of New Berlin is bad architecture, or that the cooking in the big cosmopolitan hotels is bad cooking. But the passages of his good rhetoric are amazing. In this same *Dombey and Son* the little passage at the beginning, Mrs. Dombey holding her daughter as she dies, is at the highest level; it does exactly what rhetoric ought to do, it produces the emotion of verse, while retaining, though transfigured, the form of prose.

In the matter of morals (which must always be examined in any writer, for they inform his writing and are the very body of what he writes) Dickens seems to me singularly sound, save in one particular. And I would put it to this test, that his morals felt sound in his own time, feel sound to us to-day, and will feel sound, I think, one hundred years hence, or as long time further as he may endure.   There is throughout a dislike of falsehood in statement, an accuracy in proportion—that is, in distinguishing the important from the unimportant where right and wrong are concerned—and also a burning zeal for justice which is very rare in writers of any kind; more common, though also rare, in speakers.

But in this department of morals Dickens seems to me to have one great area of weakness.   He lapses into that worst of heresies, the Gospel of Kindliness.   He cannot be blamed; it was of his time.   He lived in that generation when the old transcendental faith of Englishmen was beginning to break down (it has long ago disappeared), and he clung to such fragments of it as could still appeal to the heart.   In truth, this Gospel of Kindliness is an abomination before the Lord.   This gospel of easy charity and nothing else mattering is the very essence of topsy-turvydom in moral values; for it refuses to inquire why a good deed is good or what it is which makes it a good deed; and it reduces all judgment in such things to the basest of tests, a sort of comfortable warmth. At bottom all those morals are the morals of confusion. Thus I confess that, for my part, I can hardly read the pages dealing with the Cheeryble Brothers: not because they are obviously out of nature—all Dickens is that, and I don't mind it a bit; so long as the creator of puppets makes them live and amuses me he is fulfilling his function—but the Cheerybles do not amuse me, they only nauseate me. I am told that *Little Nell* is even worse. I have not come to her yet in my re-reading.

But with that, having said what is true, that these puppets are unreal and that their intense life is life given them by their author and not by nature, I would close with one more statement which I believe to be true—though I again beg my readers to believe that all such personal effects of a writer upon a reader are very limited and not to be trusted. It seems to me that Dickens has a marvellous faculty for seizing certain permanent characteristics present in certain classes. It is all very well to laugh at his aristocrats and to say that they do not resemble aristocrats. They do not. They no more resemble aristocrats than the Pavilion at Brighton resembles the architecture of the Orient. But he has got the very heart of the permanent aristocratic foibles. He has appreciated as no one else has, out of a great number of talented men and even men of genius who have dealt with it, the superb irony of the London populace. He gets exactly, to the hundredth of an inch, the motives of hypocrisy and vanity in our average selves. And that is an amazing achievement for a man whose sentimentalism ran so false, and who, having no tradition behind him, let alone any systematic philosophy and religion, had no guide to keep him in touch with reality.

VII

On the Tears of the Great

'Sunt Lachrymae Rerum et Mentem mortalia tangunt.'
Old Saw.

AND WHAT IS THAT FOSSIL TAG TO THE POINT?
WHY, NOT AT ALL. FOR WHATEVER "RERUM"
may mean (and there are sixteen versions), Great
Men it certainly is not. Why, then, do I set it
down at the head of this? Why, because a man
must make the most of whatever little Latin or
Greek he has, and this is the only lachrymal line
running in my head for the moment. Moreover,
one of the chief rules in using tags is that they
should be thoroughly well vulgarised and polished
and known to the whole world. The other, converse,
dodge used with some effect, of trotting out bits of
Latin and Greek no one has ever heard of, is effective
with the simple—but it is very dangerous; and that
for two reasons: your reader suspects you of having
made them up, and you will probably get them
wrong.

Now it is not so with William Shakespeare. You may quote from Shakespeare anything you like, and it will always pass muster, however bad, or commonplace, or silly, or profound. Was it not in this very spirit that I quoted a sham couplet of his, entirely of my own invention:

'Swift to your charges; naught was ever done
Unless at some time it were first begun.'

William did not write this; but he might have. It is just like him. It is true, and not worth telling, and it rhymes.

Nor has all this (you may remark) anything to do with strong men or their tears.

You are right; I must to my subject; although it is a hateful thing to begin any piece of work, and I never put pen to paper without wishing that I had inherited an enormous fortune, in which case you may be very certain that I should never have put pen to paper. For it was well remarked by the great Dr. Johnson that no one ever wrote save under the necessity of earning. I do not remember where the passage comes, but I suppose what he meant was that no one ever wrote anything worth reading, save for money. For certainly an enormous amount of stuff is produced by rich people who ought to know better, and who spoil the market for us poor scribblers.

And so to the tears of Great Men: for it is time that I embarked upon this subject. Not, indeed, that it is a very engaging one to your eyes, for the spectacle of a Great Man boohooing and blubbering and playing the cry-baby must be very distressing to you: at any rate, it is distressing to most moderns. Our fathers thought nothing of it, and you will remark till right down into the middle of the nineteenth century men weeping copiously; in literature, at least. I suppose the prejudice against it, like so many other startlingly modern differences from the past, is due to the public schools. Anyhow, there it is, and for my part I hope it will not last for long. I like the older habit. I want to see the grimacing and the puckering and to hear the sobs again.

For if you will think of it, all history is full of such tears. And it is the greatest men who weep the loudest. The heroes roared upon all occasion, in every tragedy, epic and ballad. I think it was Arnold of Rugby who came along and stuffed the middle classes with a new and a worse repression. David wept for Absalom, and even for Saul; and after a certain lapse of time he even wept for Uriah. He was proud of his sobbing and set it down in writing. Moses wept upon three occasions, and Jacob once or twice. And Adam, our common father, I suppose must have wept, or we should not have inherited the habit. While as for Jeremiah, he was a very fountain of tears.

But to pass from Holy Writ to the profane authors, have we not it in Homer's *Iliad* (the 21st Book) that Priam wept before Achilles in pleading for the body of Hector—advocate's tears! And Achilles himself, as witness Book 18 or Sigma, wept for Patroclus. Nay, the very horses of these Captains were so haunted by the current fashion that they copied their masters and wept in addressing their father Jove, as you may read in the same work, but in the 6th Book. Augustus wept when the Mantuan read out to him in a grave voice the *Tu Marcellus Eris,* and Naso wept most sincerely on hearing of his condemnation to exile. St. Austin wept for his sins. Caracalla out of sheer rage, and Marcus Aurelius from priggishness—or perhaps from a puny sentiment on hearing what a fool his wife had made of him.

Then have we not the tears of Scipio as he watched the fall of Carthage? And even as they fell, Scipio with your Great Man's passion for the tag came out with the most hackneyed quotation that he could recall—perhaps he knew no other—moaning

'There will come a day when Holy Ilium itself shall perish,' etc., etc.

Coriolanus wept when he saw his mother—a forbidding woman; and Pluto, Lord of Hell, wept when Orpheus played to him that lovely phrase from Gluck—but these were iron tears.

Alexander wept, though sober at the time, because he thought he had no more worlds to conquer. It was gross ignorance in him. There was still the north of India, all China, all the Western Mediterranean, including Tangitana and the golden light of the Hesperides, the Germans, the Britons and Gaul, and the immense spaces of Scythia. But he did well to leave these last alone, for they bring no luck, whether to Napoleon or to our English novelists. Indeed, I never knew anyone who ever made an attack on Russia, whether by arms or by interview, who did not come to grief. Witness Prussia only the other day, the grave danger of Poland a few years ago, and the unfortunate history of the Grand Turk.

Charlemagne wept to see pirate barques upon the sea, and St. Gregory the Great on hearing that a poor man had starved to death in the streets of Rome

—a subject which would move us to-day, who are more enlightened, rather to laughter than to tears.

The great nobles gathered about the death-bed of Louis XIV wept bitterly, so eloquent was his last discourse; and he gravely begged their pardon for having thus disturbed their dignity. King Lear (it is true he is but a fellow in a book) wept copiously. But it was his own fault, as his Fool told him. If he had made Goneril and Regan weep in youth it would have been more to his purpose in age. Hubert de Burgh in the same fiction weeps, and so does the melancholy Jacques; and if I am not mistaken, Mr. Allworthy wept upon at least one occasion in *Tom Jones*.

The anthology is full of great poets who follow suit; like the one who wept for Heraclitus, and the other greater one (greater although too softly Syrian) who wept for Heliodora.

But, indeed, all the poets in chorus have worked tears to death.

How often have they not written the opening words, 'Weep not for me,' which no one, by God! had the least intention of doing. Yet if I go on with the poets I shall be side-tracking myself and getting among the angels and the jackasses; so let me return to the Great Men.

Cromwell was perpetually bursting into tears. He sniffed and rubbed his eyes to see Charles the king with his children. Tears rolled down his cheeks in prayer, and again in domestic bereavement. He was one of the great criers of history, an unfailing and repetitive, as it were, chain-weeper. The second of the noble Hanoverians, whom I suppose I may call a Great Man, for he was of Nordic stock and reasonably rich, cried when his wife died; Dr. Johnson at the memory of his mother, Pitt the Younger upon the news of Austerlitz, and under the effect of port; Macaulay (I am told) at the discovery of a stumer cheque. Thiers wept when he signed the capitulation to Bismarck, and the Moltke of the last war when there reached him at head-quarters in Luxemburg the news of the Marne. Alfred, Lord Tennyson, Laureate, wept, or at least allowed the tears to gather to his eyes, at the prospect of stubble in the English country-side. Carlyle wept when he thought of his wife after her death, and his wife when she thought of Carlyle before it. Louis XVI wept because he was hen-pecked, and Louis XV because he had no such luck. But Louis XVIII, if he wept at all, wept only through the excruciating agony of the gout.

With all this mass of example behind you, may

48

you not conclude that the new-fangled fashion of swallowing one's tears and restraining one's sorrow, and of affecting a stony countenance, has no long life before it?

I suppose I shall not live to see the return of tears, but men who are young to-day will live to see it; men high in the places of Government, Cabinet Ministers (if there are still such creatures forty years hence), will publicly ululate upon losing a lucrative commercial position; speculators will break down in the club as they watch the adverse tape; and popular authors will caterwaul when they read the reviews written upon them by reasonably well-educated men.

I shall not live, I say, to see that recrudescence of a very honest, very necessary human habit; but it will come, and meanwhile I seek consolation in this, as in every other matter, from the glories of the past: from the Classic Muse.

VIII

On Labels

MANY YEARS AGO I HEARD FROM THE LIPS OF A WISE WOMAN, WHO HAD KNOWN MOST OF her generation, that it would be great fun to keep an album in which there should be on one side of the page what public men were really like, and on the other side the *label* attached to them as public men: the idea that the public had been given of them. The difference is sometimes startling, always very great, often grotesque.

I am prepared to maintain that the divergence between the reality and the effigy is far greater to-day than it has been in the past, and much greater in England than it is in any other country. And I am prepared to maintain the apparent paradox that this is due to the effect of the Press acting upon dense urban populations; all able to read, but now ground into a dust without corporate bond. But whether I be right or wrong in this, all will admit

that there *is* this very sharp and wide distinction between the real man and the imaginary public person.

I remember reading, as a boy, in a book then
famous, and still, I suppose, jogging along—I mean
The Autocrat of the Breakfast Table—a repetition
(as though it were new) of the old joke that when
two people were in conversation there were really
six present. It was a statement not new to the world,
but new to me. Youth is innocent and just, and I
spotted the error at once. There are not six people
present—there are four. The idea that there were
six people is based on the conception that a man is not
really known to himself, so that in such a conversation you have A as he really is, A as he thinks he is,
A as B thinks he is—and the same triple series for B,
which makes six people in all. But that is bad
philosophy. What a man thinks he is, that he is.
There are only four people present in any conversation between two. The real A, and B's idea of A;
the real B, and A's idea of B. If any man, woman
or even child, being of reasonable age and responsible for his or her actions, civil or canonical, religious
or lay, public or domestic, make so bold as to differ
from this my affirmation by so much as a hair's
breadth, may he, she or it be anathema. Which reminds me of the Tale of the Tub—but were I to

follow up everything I am reminded of when I write, what I write would go to pieces. So to return.

There are, then, *four* people present in every conversation; but at least in such conversation there is direct contact. B can judge of A more or less, and A of B. B does not take A to be twenty-five when A is really forty; nor alert when he is sodden. But the difference between the label of the public man and the public man himself may be a difference of almost any degree.

The photographs of the great on which the wretched millions are fed belong to half a lifetime before the day on which they are seen.

One of the few mournful pleasures in life is to look down the most vulgar of all the vulgar columns, the column dealing with the private habits of the rich (which are really nobody's concern), and there see that Lady Wuzz has gone to Howling Towers, while Sir Henry Buzz has done the clean contrary thing and left the Historic House. You shall have a picture of either of these people—Lady Wuzz as her face wuzz in those dear days when one could lounge down Piccadilly and all London was full of horses, and when gentlemen were to be seen in the flesh: Sir Henry Buzz as he was just after the Boer War, when he became rich enough to get photographed, but not yet rich enough to buy anybody's soul—cheap as that article is when caught in the right place and time.

Then there is the point of emphasis. The real man is a maze of a million notes: the label is all on one note. Politicians know this well, and so do their twin brethren, the comic actors of the Music Hall stage. One must have a particular kind of hat; another must smoke a pipe; a third must be represented eating a potato, because he may have said in one speech that he liked potatoes. A fourth will be given a red nose, or big ears, or whatever else is necessary for Modern Glory. And as with the body, so with what used to be called the soul (whatever that may be). Your public man is a human being after all. He is, therefore, complex. He is organic. He has in each emotion a myriad strings, on which the angels and the demons play. But his effigy, his label, is bound to some one emotion, and one only—or, at the most, two. He is a man who is always either hitting balls with a bat, or always riding a horse, or always making the same wearisome speech about the same wearisome thing, or always holding his hands like the paws of a listening rabbit sitting on its tail, or mysteriously brooding over his next swindle, or painting a picture all the time, or writing verse all the time, or preaching all the time.

There is also downright falsehood in the label of the Public Man: the effigy of a man quite different from what he was, even in some obvious physical characteristic. Lord Randolph Churchill, for instance, was a tall man; nine out of ten thought him a short man, because his caricatures were drawn upon that style.

With talents or with essential qualities of character it is far worse. I have listened to most of the public speakers of my time, and I can say with perfect sincerity, and with unshakeable confidence in my own judgment—what is more, with a certitude that all fresh minds would agree with me—that not one in ten can speak at all. They pour out a mass of worthless stuff, unorganised, not even intended to be true, as a matter of routine, repetitive, filling time; but they are labelled 'orators.'

We all know what eloquence is; we all remember the rare occasions in life when we have heard it. I have not yet heard it from a professional public speaker.

I have heard it in moments of sincere anger in

private life; I have heard it often enough in the pulpit. Especially have I heard it on those rare occasions when an individual man of high talent, hating publicity, thinks it his duty to come out and speak (at great peril to himself) and get himself heard. But I have never heard it yet from the people who have to grind out political speeches: after all, that is what one would expect. Yet the idea that they speak well is part and parcel of the label attaching to those who are known for public speeches.

There is one exception: the man who is so hopeless that he cannot speak at all—that he is like an animal. If he be a public man through hereditary position, or through some accident of fortune, he is praised for *not* being eloquent; in the place of eloquence he is labelled 'common-sense'—and after all, this Swinish Sort do less harm than their Foxy colleagues.

The State suffers by this divergence between the label and the man. It interferes greatly with the multiplicity of talented effort. The label will have a man to be a poet or a wit or a financier; it will therefore have all his verse good; all his sayings witty; all his judgments in finance sound. And, on the top of that, it will make it as difficult as possible

55

for him to exercise any other functions than those to which the label applies.

Now in private life, where we really can judge men, we know not only that high multiplicity of talent is common, but that some multiplicity of function is invariably found in every character; and we also know that without such multiplicity of function our association with our fellows would be intolerable. Fancy a man who never opened his mouth without making a joke! Or whom we had to associate with daily, but who could only play conjuring tricks!

All falsehoods do harm, but this particular falsehood does the grave and increasing harm to the State of wasting service. When there is a crisis the wrong man is given the job—because of the label. The right man is unknown because of the label. I remember a case in point, where a man of good birth and of ancient name who had been made a director of a company because of his name, and who was supposed to be no more than an ornament, took over the management, and turned the thing from failure to success. He might have done it fifteen years earlier and have saved a quantity of widows and orphans and parsons I know not how many thousands, had it not been that his colleagues had labelled him a born Lord and had forgotten that there was no particular reason why a born Lord should not be able to organise.

Let me conclude with this comforting reflection. Like all our modern evils, this evil will not get better. It will get worse. The only remedy for our modern evils is catastrophe.

IX

On the Fall of Lucifer

EVERY SERMON SHOULD HAVE A TEXT. THIS IS MY TEXT; IT IS TAKEN FROM A NEWSPAPER account of a sale of pictures:

> 'Only two prices had a respectable appearance, forty-two guineas for a large cartoon of "David and Solomon" and eighty-two guineas for "The Fall of Lucifer," a water-colour in a bluish tinge, measuring ninety-seven inches by forty-nine and three-quarters.'

I read it a week ago. It was much the most remarkable piece of news I had read for many days. It eclipsed the abuse of the Poor, of the French, of the Poles; it even eclipsed the self-praise of the rest of the paper. It stood right out in front of my mind as vivid as a tiger. I wanted to travel to the distant place of which the story was told and to see the thing with my own eyes—'The Fall of Lucifer,' no less than ninety-seven inches one way and within a quarter of an inch of fifty inches the other!

Note you, this is some water-colour! I am inaccurate by nature, but I think that ninety-seven inches is eight feet one inch; bigger than a giant: a water-colour that would have to go sideways through an ordinary door.

I am taking it for granted that 'The Fall of Lucifer' is tall rather than long. After all, he fell three (or nine) times the space that measures day and night, according to Milton, who had more inside knowledge of the details than anybody else, and one does not see how an Archangel can fall sideways. It seems common sense that he should fall downwards, like anybody else. So I take it that somewhere in the world there exists this glorious thing, about as big as a French window or the chassis of a Rolls-Royce, and representing what I, for my part, regard as the best moral story in the world, showing the consequences of misuse in the matter of freewill.

Do I weary you when I emphasise the thing once more? When I say that the thing was a *water-colour*, not oil or tempera? It would not be so astonishing in oil, nor even in tempera. There are frescoes in oils, such as 'Judgment' and 'Temptation of St. Anthony,' and presentation portraits of Lord Mayors and Cabinet Ministers on that scale. Not that all mayors and Cabinet Ministers are eight feet high; and what is more, they are usually painted sitting down, because they are usually of an age when one gets tired standing up for hours in a dull studio. But the picture will be often enough eight feet high, especially if it is of the old-fashioned sort; with a marshal caracolling on his horse it may be higher still. But a *water-colour* of this size I never heard of —and I never thought to hear of such a thing in my life at all till I read this marvellous piece of prose.

Then there is the 'bluish tinge.' It fetched me from the moment my eyes fell upon it. Usually your 'Fall of Lucifer' is a study in black and red. Lucifer is black, or at any rate dark brown, and the flames dancing about are red.

There are exceptions. I know of one in Paris where an exceedingly well-groomed St. Michael is sticking (without effort) an exceedingly annoyed devil with curly hair and of a sanguine complexion, not even southern. But how they managed to make him *blue*, and the fibre blue as well, is more than I can understand. Perhaps they caught the fall half-way, or at the beginning, while Lucifer was still nearer Heaven than Hell, and we all know that the natural colour of Heaven is blue. Or perhaps the idea was to convey the truth that Lucifer is a spirit.

Spirits are usually represented as a sort of bluish-white, and they look much more real on the stage when they incline to that colour.

Anyhow, there it is—ninety-seven inches by fifty (save a quarter of an inch) and showing a mighty theme upon a mighty scale. Unless, indeed, the newspaper lies—which I am loath to believe.

There is another oddity about this wonderful piece of news. No name is given of the artist. We are informed in the same paragraph that a whole cart-load of Burne-Jones's went for a few pounds—which does not surprise me—and that a Holman Hunt went for a guinea and a half. But neither in the case of 'David and Solomon' (a cartoon) nor in the case of their predecessor 'Lucifer' (of a bluish tinge) are we given the name of the artist.

Now, in my view, that is something most astonishing. Here is your 'Fall of Lucifer' estimated at about twenty-seven times the value of your Holman Hunt, and apparently ten or twelve times the value of your Burne-Jones—and yet not a hint upon its creator!

Was it humility, as with the author of the *Imitatio?* Or reason of state, as with Bacon, the author of *Hamlet?* Or mere fate, as with Homer, the author of *Homer?* Was it ignorance of his own value, as with the author of *Wuthering Heights?* Or dread of criticism, as with the author of *Waverley?* Or mere routine, as with the architect of Amiens? Or terror, as with the author of *Lloyd George in Peace and War?*

Then there is the price: the high price. What made that price, I wonder? Eighty-two mortal guineas! Eighty-four pounds and (I think) two shillings! Was it the sheer unqualified appetite of the bidder for the subject, or was it that ninety-seven inches by forty-nine and three-quarters exactly fitted a panel in his house? Or was he perhaps a Fundamentalist, an Anglo-Saxon (as Americans are sometimes called) who had never heard of anything outside his paternal theology? Were the pictures sold in a place to which Burne-Jones's name had not penetrated and where models with pushed-in faces were unpopular, but Scripture still supreme?

Stay! Your Fundamentalist would know nothing about 'The Fall of Lucifer.' I may be wrong, but I can recollect no passage in the Holy Writ giving even the outline of that affair. I believe it to be purely traditional. There are hints at it in Scripture, I know, but I can recollect no straightforward reference, however short. It is otherwise with 'David and

Solomon.' They are plumb Biblical figures. But I feel doubtful about Lucifer—under that name.

Those who have the sense to know their Le Sage by heart will remember how, in *The Devil on Two Sticks*, the Student trying to be polite to the Demon asks him whether he is not one of the great major devils, and courteously suggests Beelzebub, Ashtaroth, and half a dozen other names, until his interlocutor interrupts him with annoyance and says, 'Be silent! I see you know nothing of High Society in Hell!'

The story has always warned me to be careful in laying down the rank and position of any Devil, but I think I am on safe ground when I say that Lucifer is the chief one.

There are other Lucifers, I know. There is that good bishop who (with Hilary his deacon) defended St. Athanasius somewhat too warmly. Then there is the Morning Star, and (for that matter) the fellow who used to go the rounds with a long pole, lighting the gas lamps of London when I was young. He goes his rounds no more.

But I take that Lucifer of the picture sale to be *the* Lucifer, *Ille Lucifer*, the Phosphorus. I argue it from the word 'Fall'—and I wish I had seen it!

63

X

On Epigrams

'Sing, Heav'nly Muse,'
I sing—no, I prose—of Epigram.

NOTE, WHEN I SAY EPIGRAM, I MEAN EPIGRAM IN VERSE. THE MOMENT YOU BEGIN TO TALK of other epigrams, you are without limits or bounds: you are without form and void, as was the earth before the biologists tackled it and made it the jolly thing it is through their very powerful instrument of Natural Selection. There is nothing more wearisome than discussing things which are without form and void, or, for that matter, than looking at them. Therefore I say that when I write of epigram I write of epigram in verse.

Now, I do not deny that epigram can be written in prose; indeed, the great mass of epigram has been so written, from the time when the first man who murdered his brother by stealth said (in the language of those parts), 'You did not catch the irony of my last remark,' to the words which some say are those of a modern Pope, who remarked to the English Bishop of Gibraltar, 'I also am conspicuous in your diocese.' But the human race has agreed—I hope, and if they have not, they must agree after the publishing of this essay, for they will have no choice— that the perfect epigram must be in verse.

The reason is that all things attain perfection through form, and that in form is their perfection defined. Now verse is the triumph of form. On which account have I always regarded prose as the lumbering, terrestrial, blear-eyed, stumble-footed, gasping, unsatisfactory, bestial, lower-than-half-brother, terrene, second-cousin downwards, of verse.

Of poesy I do not speak; that is matter for gods: but I say that plain verse is the necessary vehicle of any perfect form.

On this account also (I know very well that I am digressing—but so I must) I believe that all compositions in their perfection should be in verse. Thus a Collins, after a week-end in the country, should run:

'Thank you, my Friend, who have a lot of oof,
For keeping me two nights beneath your roof.'

The love-letter:

> 'It was my shame, and now it is my boast,
> That I have loved you rather more than most.'

The invitation:

> 'If you will lunch with me at half-past one,
> You'll meet Maria's unimportant son.'

The excuse:

> 'I cannot dine upon the thirty-first,
> Because I suffer from a normal thirst,
> And what you give your guests is of the worst.'

Here I must digress again, adding a digression within a digression, like those brackets within brackets which are the delight of examiners in algebra. It is a mistake to make 'thirst' rhyme with 'first,' because 'th' is too much like 'f' in sound. On the other hand, there are not enough rhymes in that monosyllable 'urst' or 'irst.' Indeed, it is a defect of the English language that there should be so few rhymes in it. This defect has been very well pointed out by Captain Grahame in his lines about Love Poetry.

I now end this digression within a digression and go back to the matter of my original digression.

(I confess we are getting a long way off from epi-grams; but it is my pride to return at last, like the boomerang, to the place from which I started.)

All forms of expression are at their highest in verse. Not in rhyme, note you, which is a pecu-liarity of our civilisation; but in a strict and ritually rhythmic shape.

Look at this, for instance, which is the motto of the magazine of my old school:

'Tanti non es ais, sapis Luperce.'

End of the digression.

The epigram in verse tests the writer. He must pull it off altogether, or not at all. The epigram in prose may succeed or half-succeed, and there is no boundary between the one and the other; but the success and the half-success fade away over an in-definite belt. You can never say of the epigram in prose, 'This is final! This is It!' But you can of the epigram in verse.

When you read, for instance, of the Divines who:

'Tried to learn polite behaviour
By reading books against their Saviour'

(I hope I have got it right: it is something like that, anyhow), you may justly say that the target has been touched in the bull's-eye. Here is finality. Here is a stone wall. And so you may say, I think, of the couplet:

> 'He would often flush with terror, where another would have paled;
> And he tried to do his duty—but how damnably he failed!'

or again:

> 'Godolphin says he does not wish to swell
> The Roll of Fame; and it is just as well.'

There has come into being during our own time a very damnable sort of man, bred I know not under what influences, and cursed by I know not what malignant Stars, having about his cradle at his baptismal feast Evil Fairies crowding the Good, and enchanted by the Wizard Enemies of his father, or perhaps of his mother; there is a sort of man, I say, who attempts epigram—yes, and epigram in verse!—without the least conception of what is meant by finality. He seems to think (does this Abortion—I use the term in its most general sense) that so long as the joke is obvious, the syllables in each line of the required number, and the couplet or quatrain rhyming, he has written an epigram. Frankly, I prefer the fellow who is content with the tiresome old dodge of taking a common saying, turning it upside down, issuing it thus in prose, and so achieving fame from Wimbledon, passing round by the south through Croydon to Eltham, Lewisham, Greenwich, and so across the river by East Ham, Islington (I suppose— I have but a vague idea of the map), Highgate, Hampstead, Willesden, Ealing, and in general the outer places about London.

But here again (another digression), are suburbs still suburban? Time was when a city (pronounced *Pollis*, though spelt *Polis*) was a very definite thing, full of slaves whose masters, the gentlemen, dined together and made excellent jokes. Those without the walls heard by the echoes of these, and that is why Aristophanes makes the loutish boy beg to be allowed a few 'city words' as he comes towards the Gate of Athens.

But to-day it is quite the other way. All our best wits live in the suburbs, and indeed, on account of petrol and electricity, there are no suburbs to-day.

But enough of this—and to return to epigrams.

The question arises whether an epigram may ever be tender, just, loyal, pious or heroic.

It would seem not; for the epigram is a weapon made for the hand of the hater, or at the very least of the scorner.

But, on the other hand, it is written, 'God delights in Brevity,' and again, 'Be terse.' At this point I add yet another digression. It has been suggested to me even as I write. It seems there is a Board of Guardians here in London over whose doorway is inscribed this motto:

'Be brief; be bright; be gone.'

Ah me! A motto rather for youth cut off in its splendour than for guardians, who are, or were until women crept in among them, of a bearded middle age.

No, there is such a thing as your tender, or pious, even your heroic epigram; but it has to be very good indeed to stand a chance in the great press and crush of epigrams which shuffle and jostle and hustle and elbow each other down the narrow, glazed, brick-lined, bulb-lighted, tunnel-like, ill-ornamented and very stuffy corridors of our time.

Of these among the best is, I think, a line which I ascribe by memory to Hood (and if anybody else wrote it, why, let him take the glory—I shall not stand in his way):

'We thought her dying when she slept
And sleeping when she died.'

70

But this kind is not another epigram, though it also deals with the passage out of this life:

> 'Here William lies, in truth: before he died
> For forty mortal years in truth he lied!'—

yes, and steadily.

It would seem, then, that the subject of the epigram does not produce its quality, for though the subject of this last be the awful business of the transition from this mortal life to some other, yet there is nothing about it of a heroical or religious quality. It is of a baser sort.

Which reminds me, my little friends (and with this I conclude), that I did—I myself, with these mine eyes—on this very day of God, see in a tube station an advertisement stuck up in large letters, which announced me this:

> 'Swedenborg has said that Death is only the passage from this life to another.'

Lord! What an original man!

XI

If

THERE IS A SORT OF INTERJECTION COMMONLY FOUND IN HISTORICAL NARRATIVE. WE MODERNS are very fond of it, and I am in perpetual doubt whether it is justified or whether it is irrational. It is the interjection that 'if' this or that had not happened the whole course of history would have been changed. I have used it myself over and over again, because I think on the balance it is rational.

I do not mean that I think it rational only because I regard the scheme of things as fluid. I do not say it only because the monistic philosophy of to-day with its facile conception of inevitable sequence and of unchanging law seems to me foolish, but also because great special accidental factors do stand out in history.

It is true that the number of things which would have changed all history at any one moment is great. You may say that if a certain person had not arrived at a certain moment in a certain place such and such

a battle would have had another issue, or that such
and such a policy would not have been decided on,
but a great many other things besides this man's appearing in that particular place and time would also
have changed the future. It is true that if the Royal
Family had not been stopped at Varennes by a margin of five minutes; if Drouot had started five minutes later, or if his horse had failed on that dark
night in the wood, the French monarchy would not
have fallen. But it is also true that it would not
have fallen if Choiseul had waited a few minutes
more at the posting house, or if Louis XVI had
taken less time over lunch, or if the traces had not
broken. You could make a list of a dozen major
changes, and any number of minor ones, which would
have decisively affected the issue. None the less, I
incline to the judgment which uses the 'if' in history.
There is nearly always in the complicated scheme
of an event some one manifest decisive factor, and
you can usually put your finger on it by noting how
the people who want to misrepresent the affair for
their own motives of religious bias, or of patriotism,
or of gain, are concerned to explain away this one
factor.

For instance, the main factor in the failure of the
Armada was the wind. Had the summer not been

73

an exceptional one of furious gales the Armada would have come back nearly intact. Had the wind not blown heavily from the west, at the most critical moment from the north-west, and backed to a gale, the Armada would not have run up the Straits after its first confusion. Our patriotic feeling has of late attempted to minimise this factor, yet it was certainly the decisive factor. The English ships were better for their jobs than the Spanish ships were for theirs. They sailed closer to the wind, they carried heavier metal, they were better munitioned. They did not fire too high when they leaned over to the wind, so that even if they had not had the wind gauge their fire would have told more heavily than the opponent's. Again, if Parma had had all his troops ready to embark, and had had free use of the ports, he might have got them on board in time— it is just possible. Again, if the Armada had not met its first bad gale after starting, and had not had to go back to refit, it would not have come in for that bad patch of weather at the end of July. Nevertheless, it remains true that the wind on these later July days was the decisive factor, and the moderns do ill to try to correct contemporaries who saw that it was so, and who very properly constructed for

74

their medal the phrase that God had sent His wind and had dispersed them.

In the same way the breaking of ranks from Harold's line at Hastings was decisive. If there had been modern discipline and they had been held in hand the defensive would have won. There were a great many other factors. There was a difference in armament, there was the fatigue of that enormous march from London, but I think the main factor was the breaking of the line in the first abortive and partial charge downhill. Harold's men got ' 'foreside,' and were surrounded and cut up; when William saw that that was the result of any such breaking in the line he used it, though that he did so by deliberate ruse on his own account, I doubt. It reads more like boasting after the event. It is more likely that he watched that renewal of the error on the part of his opponents whenever his own line wavered and took immediate advantage of it.

I suppose of all modern decisions nothing has made more difference to the history of the world than the decision of the English Cabinet not to recognise the Southern States as an independent nation during the American Civil War. We have heard very many accounts explaining this, notably the account which puts down so much to Prince Albert. I have heard one account, which I believe to be true, because I have it by direct oral tradition with only two intermediaries between myself and the original actors: and both intermediaries were educated gentlemen, were in the heart of what governs (or used to govern) England, and were truthful men. And oral tradition of this kind is worth far more as historical evidence than is any official document. Here, then, is another of those 'ifs.'

What I heard was this. The Prime Minister and the Cabinet had determined to recognise the Southern States, but the publication of the decision had to be postponed. Gladstone going up to Newcastle blurted out the phrase that 'Jeff Davis had created a Nation,' and this premature declaration ruined the Cabinet's plan.

It may be so. It seems in these matters you have to judge the value of evidence after a fashion different from the way in which you judge it in daily life, let alone in a record. Not only is all your evidence at third, fourth or fifth hand, but you have to decide without knowing the people concerned as we know contemporaries: of whom we can judge whether they are telling the truth. That is why the best evidence of all in history is the evidence of those who do not mean to give evidence—chance allusions, or, better still, the evidence of inanimate objects.

But to return to the 'if.' If Calvin had not written his book there would have been no organised counter-Church in France. The confused original movement would not have had a nucleus and a framework, and 'The Religion,' as they called it, would hardly have had corporate existence. From that a whole train of consequences would have arisen which would have meant a completely different history for Europe in the seventeenth and eighteenth centuries. If the Arouet family had not suffered misfortune at the hands of the officials and of the Church, Voltaire would not have written as he did. And if there had not been the writings of Voltaire, would there have been the successful attack on religion which marked the eighteenth century and laid a foundation for all the discords of the nineteenth? I doubt it.

Or take another little point. We have the poems of Catullus, I am told, through only three manuscripts and those not very old ones. Suppose the late copiers of an earlier manuscript had not undertaken those particular tasks, or suppose their parchments had been lost or burned, we should no more have the work of Catullus than we have that of

77

Calvus. Or supposing that the immense odds against the Montfort had been successful at Muret, the South of France would have remained Albigensian and probably in time the rest of the French civilisation would have followed. But, then, for the matter of that, I suppose that if Mahomet had been thrown off his camel hard enough as a young man, we should not have had a revolution that has affected half the world.

Should we have had a very great change in history if Cæsar had failed to land on the beach at Hadrumetum, which is Sousse? Most people would say No, for anyhow Cæsar was later murdered, and whatever had happened the Civil Wars would have taken place. The same factors would have emerged and the Empire was inevitable. But I confess for my part I distrust, as I have said, this inevitableness of history. If you want to accept it you have to accept, before you have done your thinking out of the matter, the inevitableness of every detail in cause and effect, and that is a philosophy which a knowledge of life destroys.

By the way, talking of these 'ifs,' I wonder how many people see the point of the false epigram about Cleopatra's nose? Everybody has heard (I don't know who first said it) that if Cleopatra's nose had been a little longer the history of the world would have been very different. So it would; but the point of the remark is that Cleopatra's nose was already quite out of nature. If the bust we have is genuine her nose was already so long and curved as to be monstrous. It makes you think of a parrot. And talking of noses, if John Churchill's nose had been a putty one, or snub nose, or bulbous nose, that very handsome young man would not have enjoyed the disgraceful beginnings of his career: and I am quite certain that without John Churchill the Allies would never have enjoyed their final victories. It was not his early start that gave John Churchill his genius, but it was his early start that enabled him to use that genius.

Then, again, if Edward IV had been drowned when he was making that amazing voyage up the Channel as a boy of nineteen (not sufficient honour has been paid to his courage) I suppose a Lancastrian dynasty would have remained securely on the throne. Descendants of the Tudor group would never have reigned, and we might have had a popular monarchy to this day. But, then, for that matter, at the very beginning of the Civil Wars had there been a Napoleon or a Turenne on the King's side, the Civil Wars might have ended in the first

79

weeks and the impoverished monarchy of the English might conceivably have recovered.

If Columbus had been beaten back by a couple of heavy storms at the end of that voyage, would the New World have been found? I think it would, for adventure was everywhere in that day, and someone would have done the work; but the benefit might not have fallen to Spain, it might have fallen to the French monarchy.

If someone had not ill-advised Philip II to impose a ten per cent. turn-over tax upon the Netherlands, *that* would have changed all history. If some man weaker than the rest had given way to the demands of the Colonists in 1774, *that* would have changed all history. A little wisdom and a little tenacity have often ruined a cause which mere folly and weakness would have saved. There are those who will tell you also that if the Statue of Victory had not been removed from the Senate House the western Roman centralisation would not have collapsed. It is superstitious to believe this, and therefore I believe it; but I do not expect anyone else to, and I will not press the point. All I can say is that, in the event, the pagans had a perfect right to say, 'I told you so.'

If Boniface had not called in the Vandals to North Africa in a fit of pique, all history would have been changed, and if those two petty generals of the Roman forces with their two little commands, Syagrius and Clovis, had had different luck, if Syagrius had beaten Clovis, who knows but that the Western world might be Arian (and collapsed) to-day?

And so on. The most interesting thought of all in this connexion is that in our own presence there may pass some little unimportant passage, some street accident, some change in the weather, which shall prove to the future historian a turning point; and that 'ifs' are passing before us unnoticed in our own time.

Therefore, let us determine not to care and to decide that we can do nothing; only remember that if we make such a decision we shall regret it.

XII

On 'Vathek'

THERE ARE BOOKS OF THE FIRST EXCELLENCE WHICH ARE YET FORGOTTEN, NOT A LIFETIME after their first enthusiastic recognition. Sometimes their names are remembered and are quoted often enough by people who have never read a line of them. Among the last is *Vathek*. *Vathek* does not take the place which belongs to it in the story of English letters, still less has it the place which belongs to it as a particular, a unique thing.

Yet in the whole range of English literature there are but two short stories (in the old sense of the word 'short story,' not a magazine article, but a completed piece of fiction) which can take their rank with the fifty or more of the French model from which they derive. These two are *Rasselas* and *Vathek*. Everyone should read them. They ought to be common text-books with which the youth of England were as familiar as they are with too much of the lesser stuff in Shakespeare, and the whole wads of text-book fodder ladled out to them for specimens of their country's achievements.

Of the two books *Rasselas* is the greater, yet *Vathek* the more remarkable. *Rasselas* weighs more, but *Vathek* is the more incisive. It ought to count with that very different book *Wuthering Heights* as a triumph in deep etching. No one who has read it ever forgets it, or can cast out of his mind the branded lesson which it conveys.

Like *Rasselas*, *Vathek* was written at a sitting. Indeed, both books convey that powerful sense of unity which is of such value in the founding of any work; and it is unity of a sort which comes through immediate action of the pen when the mind of the writer is at its highest potential. But unlike *Rasselas*, *Vathek* was written *literally* at a sitting, if we are to believe its author (and I see no reason why we should not). That is *Vathek* was written without its author stirring from his work, his mind wholly absorbed in it, and with no distraction of meal or sleep or converse. *Rasselas* was, if I remember right, continuously written; indeed, but a matter of a few days. It is worth remembering that while both books are upon the high French model of the eighteenth century (as was, for that matter, the verse of the time), *Rasselas* was a purely English production. It is as national a book as you could find in the language. But *Vathek*, a triumph though it is of English prose, was written originally in French: so scholarly and so adaptable was that generation of educated Englishmen.

Indeed, the fate of *Vathek* in the matter of language is as interesting as it is curious. Its author, Beckford, perhaps the wealthiest man of his time, the son of a Lord Mayor of London, amused himself by writing the famous thing in the French tongue. For this kind of story had been presented to English minds in the French medium, and Beckford, when he flashed out the work, must have been fresh from the reading of Diderot and Voltaire. Presumably he did not care whether it were known or not; he seems to have had no intention of ever printing it.

But a clergyman who was with him saw the manuscript, translated it into English, and it is this English version which we have to-day.

Here is, indeed, an extraordinary historical incident, and one which makes a man think curiously (and I hope profoundly) upon the genius of language. A piece of work is written by an Englishman in the French tongue. It is so much admired by another Englishman that this other Englishman translates it into English, and, behold, the result is a superb piece of English prose.

It is another matter worthy of consideration that the author himself, in the whole of a longish life, did nothing else by way of writing worth considering, though he was active enough in folly and vice, and that the translator left no mark whatsoever. His name remains without echo even among the minor names of English letters. Is that not a proof of inspiration? Of the truth that the best written work is not a man's own, but something granted to him from outside? I at least think so; so that it always seems to me ridiculous for any man to be vain of really first-rate written stuff, or to ascribe it to himself, or to regret the passing and loss of his power to produce it. Whether it also be ridiculous, as it would seem logically to be, that we should revere great names in literature, I know not; but, at any rate, when men cease from reverencing letters, society is doomed.

Such effects as that of *Vathek* are not produced by the subject alone, though the subject is necessary to those effects. There is needed to create these rare great things the indefinable power of style. And the style of *Vathek* is as penetrating as and more

arresting than that of Voltaire. It is English of
the contrasted, rhythmical, balanced style which the
eighteenth century spoke as its natural tongue, and
of which it made in its highest moments something
we shall not reach again.

The story of *Vathek* is of the simplest. It is the
old story of those who defy the gods; the core of all
tragedy. For tragedy is not, as has also been said,
the watching of inevitable doom in spite of man's
action. Tragedy is the picture of retribution, and
it is this which makes tragedy, like all high literary
forms, moral.

Vathek is Commander of the Faithful in the early
ages of Islam. He ridicules Divine things, and yet
(it happens to such men) has a twist for diabolism.
He is filled with a curiosity for new and vivid experience and for discovery. He would see for himself
those things which cannot be seen without supernatural aid of the wrong kind. He wishes to visit
the tombs of the Kings who reigned before Adam,
which tombs are far off in the gloomy and deserted
mountains of the Persian border. He desires to know
the dwellings of the dead. In all this he is supported
by an old witch-mother who follows his adventure
and shares his fate. He makes a compact with a
Demon who visits his court. He sets out eastward

with a great train under the promise of the reward
he has sought and he obtains it. He passes beneath
the earth to the dread sepulchres of the Monarchs
of the older time, he comes into the vast hall of
Eblis, the Ruler of Hell, and finds himself forever
damned. His old mother, his companion throughout, passes with him into that despair.

There is not in the whole range of English letters, so far as I know them, a description of the loss
of a soul compared with those last few lines of
Vathek. Indeed, it is one of the marvels of the book,
as of all first-rate work, that such an effect can be
produced with such economy of material. Read it,
and it will remain in your mind permanently: the
figures that pass, not speaking to each other, with
their eyes cast down, and each with a hand upon a
burning heart.

The course of the book—the process of its in-
cidents—leads up with an insistent mark to that
climax. You have in it all the fortunes of the soul;
its delights in this world, its repose and even its last
opportunities of salvation. Among the most poign-
ant of the brief shining passages in the work is that
where Vathek comes, in the last stages of his journey, upon a being who sings as might a shepherd
in the hills, and whose song half woos him to re-

pentance—till the Sultan determines at one last moment to continue in his evil way, and his good angel leaves him with a lamentable scream. For the book is full of freewill and is appallingly true to the realities of human life.

Remark that all this was written by one of the vilest men of his time. One whom vice drove before he died to something like madness. It was but a folly in Beckford, yet a typical folly, that he set out to build on his place at Fonthill in Wiltshire a tower higher than any other in the world. It collapsed. Of his evil nature the stories told of him, both true and false, are more illuminating.

The worst that is true of Beckford, the author, need not be repeated; but a story very typical is this one: I heard it from the child of a contemporary when I myself was young. Beckford, at Fonthill, isolated himself. Two young bloods had a bet that they would visit him against his will. They rode in and announced themselves. He kept them to dinner, promising them hospitality, but at midnight turned them into the Park, telling them that his hounds were loosed. He then bolted the door upon them, so that they fled for their lives to the nearest wood, and were rescued by hazard the next day, half-dead.

It is not an unknown accident in the history of literature that men thus doomed by their own wickedness should produce work warning others, and certainly there are few that warn more vividly than *Vathek*. It is as though the writer had been granted some presentiment of what follows the course of such living as his, had had as it were a vision, was artist enough to set the vision down, but not man enough to profit by it. At any rate, one may call *Vathek* one of the most profounding moral books of the world. Whenever I read it I recall the admirable irony of the last phrase in the parable of the Unjust Steward, 'That they may receive you into everlasting habitations.' The operative word is 'everlasting.'

There is no doubt in the mind of the reader of *Vathek*, when he lays down the book, that 'everlasting' is the just epithet for that isolation in the Hall of Eblis, those averted eyes, those hands upon those burning hearts.

XIII

On Laughter

I READ THE OTHER DAY IN A QUOTATION FROM
THE LETTERS OF LORD CHESTERFIELD (I TRUST
and hope it was from the letters) a phrase about
laughter which stuck in my memory and which, therefore, I cannot give you word for word, for the memory transforms all things; and that is its proper
province, seeing that Memory is the creator of
legend and the maker of happiness for men, causing
as she does all things to pass into a golden mist.

Well, then, as I was saying, the phrase was somewhat to this effect, 'Audible laughter is unworthy
of a gentleman, for the sound of it is unpleasant
and the contortion of the features ridiculous.' I will
not deceive you. I did not read this in the book itself, I saw it in a newspaper. I will not boast. But,
on the other hand, I will not be hypocritically hum-
ble and pretend that I have not read the Letters of
Lord Chesterfield, for I have. I bought a second-
hand copy at a bookstall in an English seaport town

a year ago. I took it out to sea with me: there I read the letters in the bunk of my little boat, and very good I found them. Lord Chesterfield seems to have been one of those men who worked like a carpenter to a mark. He did not bother himself with general ideas like Vauvenargues, or that pasty-faced Marcus Aurelius. No, he said to himself, 'What ought I to do for this unfortunate son of mine in his peculiar position—what advice ought I to give?' And he gave it (in my judgment) very well and directly.

Read him on clothes in particular; he is first-rate. I recommend every illegitimate son of a very rich and pompous father to read those letters. They are of value to us all; even to those of us who are of the base, legitimate middle classes.

Well, then, that is what Lord Chesterfield said about laughing. Perhaps he himself sometimes laughed; but he did not want his illegitimate son to laugh, and that was just as well. If I choose to laugh quite loudly or 'audibly' (as his Lordship would have said), both at Lord Chesterfield and his son, that is my business; but I warn you that I shall continue to do so, not only at Lord Chesterfield and his son, but at a good many other things: because, however much I may dislike the noise made by the laughter of others, I have no objection whatever to my own; when I perceive that this in its turn causes annoyance to third parties I remain indifferent. As for the contortion of the features, I answer, what were features made for? It is by their contortion in a greater or lesser degree that we convey emotion from soul to soul; a very noble part for any mere material things to play, and I hope the features are proud of it. Schoolboys are told that Hobbes said, 'Laughter is a sudden glory.' (I hope he did—I'm not looking it up, for the weather has turned fine again, and I am in no mood for research.) Schoolboys being told this, think it is nonsense and means nothing. They are quite right. There is a better definition of laughter which I will now give you without looking up any book. I make it up entirely out of my own head for the advantage of my fellow-beings. Note it carefully; indeed, you will do well to write it down. Genuine laughter is the physical effect produced in the rational being by what suddenly strikes his immortal soul as being damned funny. This is a first-rate definition.

Observe its admirable qualities. First of all it is circular, as all definitions should be, for the word 'funny' is a begging of the question; and since all definitions must ultimately go back to postulates which cannot be proved or themselves defined, why not begin at the beginning and make your indefinable definition at once? I see no harm in it. After all, it is what the lawyers do when they say that 'a reasonable rate of interest' is deemed to be 'a rate of interest not unreasonable under the circumstances.' Or, again, 'reasonable care' is the care which any reasonable man will take—and so on. But apart from its being circular this definition pleases me because its various parts are so beautifully adjusted.

Thus, consider the word 'sudden,' the only one in which I overlap with Hobbes. We do not laugh out loud at a joke which we have known all our lives, however good it is. We chuckle or snigger—we do not laugh. If an old gentleman slips getting out of a bus and falls down on the road, we laugh heartily. If another does the same thing five minutes later, you do not laugh so much. The third time you might even take the trouble to pick the old gentleman up and be kind to him. The fourth time the accident would seem tragic.

Again, you may read in the accounts of political speeches 'loud laughter,' but never (save in our humbugging daily papers) do you really *get* loud laughter from the politician's stage-army, unless the politician has made a more conspicuous fool of himself than usual. I have heard loud laughter at politicians in my time, but never at their jokes, which are always carefully prepared.

I remember hearing it once in the House of Commons itself—genuine, spontaneous, loud laughter. It was when a 'Distinguished Statesman'—for so he would have called himself—was attempting to pronounce the word 'abominable.' It was after dinner, and the atmosphere of the House of Commons is like nothing on earth. I do not mean that it is worse than anything on earth, although certainly as I remember it, it was worse than any other I had known. I mean that it has a secret of its own for reducing vitality. Well, anyhow, this great man tried that word 'abominable' from several points of the compass—now he tried 'Adominable,' then 'Abdominable,' 'Anonbibubble,' and anon 'Andobimoddle.' At the end he looked up, cleared his throat, and said in the most distinct resonant fashion, separating each syllable, 'Abom-in-able.' But by that time he had forgotten what it was that he had called abominable. It was all very distressing, and I hope does not happen to-day. I am talking of the bad old times of my early middle age, when the House of Commons had something ridiculous and degraded about it.

But why all this insufficient rambling stuff about

94

laughter, which I ought to have begun by compressing, as it deserves to be compressed? It is the greatest gift a man can have. Loud, happy, repeated and unrestrained laughter will never disturb a soul approaching damnation. It is not even to be found in the unhappy of this world. I except, of course, what is called forced laughter, such as the rich foolishly indulge in. As for laughter on the stage, I blame none for producing it. They have to earn their living. It is about as much like real laughter as the synthetic or imperial burgundies are like a stuff called Vosne; which, if you have not drunk it, why then you should.

I go back to my definition—laughter is provoked not only *by* what is sudden, but also *in* what is rational. I should very much like to hear the laughter of an angel, or even (if I were sufficiently armoured for that experience) the laughter of a demon. This I know, that animals do not laugh; a remark made some years before me by Rabelais, himself no mean laugher and provoker of laughter. Holy Writ, which is, on common admission, a second sort of Authority, and after its own fashion invaluable, says that dogs grin. They do. The same is true of foxes, for I have seen them do it. But no animal laughs, not even the hyena. I was in my twenty-fourth year when I went to the Zoo specially to hear whether the hyena could really laugh or not, and I spent a good deal of money which I could then ill afford, going again and again to Regent's Park until I got an opportunity. I found the hyena's effort was not a laugh at all, so that the old story about his 'being confined behind iron bars, separated from his loving mate, deprived of the use of tobacco and the daily papers, yet laugh he does, and it is greatly to his credit,' falls to the ground. The hyena's noise is a sort of violent objurgation or syncopated complaint, nothing so noble as a roar, but too proud to be a whine. Nor does the jackass laugh; it is but a proverb. The woodpecker comes nearest to it, and that is why he is called a yaffle; but he is not really laughing, he is only doing what all birds do, acting inanely without thinking, making the only noise he knows how to make, like a baby. Inanimate things, however, do laugh—waterfalls, skies under certain conditions, and, as we all know, the sea; or at any rate the Black Sea, which when you look at it westward from high enough up on the Caucasus is said to laugh 'innumerably.'

I would continue upon this subject of laughter, which is, indeed, inexhaustible (as in the species—mocking, sardonic, plaintive, imitative, sad, mean—

offensive, childish, hearty, pleasant, friendly, gentle-manly, caddish and the rest of them), did I not discover by the number of the pages whereupon this immortal fragment is inscribed that I have reached my limit.   Take it and be glad.

XIV

To the Pious and Immortal Memory of George II

WHAT A LARK IT WOULD BE IF IN THE MIDST OF ALL THESE JUBILEES, ANNIVERSARIES, centenaries, quincentenaries (if that is the right word), millenaries, seventy-fifth anniversaries, birthdays, and poppings out of discoveries, of battles and of everything in the world except the only things that really matter, they had had the grace to make a fuss about George II of England (and Elector of Hanover). There are so many all about who owe so much to him and to his family, and the bicentenary (I know that is the right word) of the little fellow's accession fell but lately, his brutish but determined father having rid himself of the world and the world of him on May 12th, 1727.

I say there are any number of people who in duty should be grateful to the pious and immortal memory of the Hanoverians, and particularly of this Hanoverian. There are the official historians, the examiners, the coaches, the great land-owning families, the parliamentarians—everybody except the mass of the people and the few cranks who pitifully bleat truth about history, drowned in the clamour of the amazing conventional lies.

It was the good health and the long reign of George II that made the Hanoverian succession certain, and the Hanoverian succession meant the destruction of the popular monarchy in these islands, and the destruction of popular monarchy meant the power of the great landlords and the squires below them, and of the industrialism which grew out of them; and all the bag of tricks. It meant the parliamentarians, it meant the trusts and monopolies, it meant plutocracy, it meant all that goes with the destruction of kingship. Quite apart from that, he was a most interesting snippet, was this man of immense lineage and farmyard manners: this typical minor German prince.

I wish I had seen him with my own eyes, strutting about, 'showing a leg' (he was proud of his little legs), with his blue, gooseberry eyes, starting out of a face like a beefsteak; his French jerked out, with, I suppose, that odd accent which all those French-speaking German gentlemen of the eighteenth century had; his absurd scraps of broken English. As for his scraps of broken English, we have record of quantities from the famous order at Dettingen to the almost equally famous stammering swearwords at Newcastle. But the one I like best (I do not know whether it is authentic—I only had it from a friend) is that which he uttered when they wakened him to tell him of his accession. He answered, I am told, half-asleep, 'Zat iss von big lie!' What a godsend for an aristocracy to have a nominal monarch of that sort to run!

I should like, too, to have seen his cock-sparrow bearing, for he was a brave little fellow, and all through history one must pay homage to courage in the male, however horrible the setting in which we find it. And poor George II was not horrible, though he was comic. He was really courageous, for he was daring in action. He was only twenty-five years of age when he charged at Oudenarde. He was sixty when he strode forward there on foot before his men against the French at Dettingen, a careless target. He deserves all the fame he got from that perfectly useless battle.

There are two other things that stand to his credit, or at least that confirm my own good opinion of him. He defended the memory of an indefensible mother, and he adored and was ruled by a very much cleverer

wife, to whom he was consistently and childishly un-
faithful—for there was a great deal that was immature in George II—and I call it immature in any
man to pout until his wife admits his mistress, and
then in gratitude at her permission to present the
lady, writes that wife a delighted letter in which he
gives details of the lady's charms! Yes, I call it
immature, because there is a lack of psychology about
it.

It is to his credit, too, that he could not stand his
father; at least, it is to the credit of his heart, though
not of his morals; for morally it is wrong, I suppose,
to treat one's father as an enemy. Anyhow, fate
caught him on the rebound, and he was punished as
he had sinned. Is it to his credit to be the father of
Hoppner, the painter? I confess frankly, I do not
know. For though all men ought to pretend to know
all about pictures, I confess I cannot do so at short
notice; so there is an end of that.

But to return to Queen Caroline: how charming
the relationship and how touching his devotion!
Everybody has heard his famous remark at her
death-bed, when she urged him to marry after she
was gone: 'Non, j' aurai des Maitresses!' What is
less famous is the dying woman's wit when she replied: 'Ah, mon dieu! cela n' empêche pas!' Still

less do people know that he insisted that, upon his own death—and after what long space of years: twenty-two mortal years and more—they should be buried together, not only in one grave, but with the sides of the coffins removed, so that they might be wedded in the tomb forever. I am touched by that in a German: still more when I remember that it was a German of the squire class, wherein one does not expect so much romance. I wonder what the man's religion was? I suppose we shall never really know. He was too stupid to be as Voltairean as his wife, and he certainly would not have been an atheist for fashion. He had none of the love of evil in all its forms which is one of the most startling characters of his immensely famous relative, Frederick the Great.

Yes, we ought to have kept the bicentenary of that round little man, and if we had I should have been at pains of making myself better acquainted with him. But the masters of the modern and rapidly-declining world in which we live have a fine nose for what truths it would be dangerous to utter to the populace. You can make heroes of a good many unpleasant people without giving the show away; but you could not make a hero of George II without even schoolboys at last understanding what it was that had replaced the ancient kingship of the English when the millionaires drove out the Stewarts.

And what form would the bicentenary have taken? They might have had little flags with a picture (in colours, I hope) of the man's face, set under a military hat. The money might have been given for the putting up of another statue of him; we have not enough ugly statues in London, nor enough dynastic ones. Nor are the streets crowded enough. Or the money might have been spent in founding a George II historical professorship at a university— the post to be open indifferently to men or women, and the duties of it being to praise without ceasing the disappearance of the Stewarts, the defeat of the Forty-five, the subsequent massacres; it might be called the Culloden Fellowship, or the Butcher Professorship (but it would be kinder to call it after the monarch in whose reign that happy event took place); and I hope that the Professor, when he or she is appointed, will make special mention of the ruin of the older Sussex families who so quixotically supported the Pretender. But, anyhow, we ought to have had this bicentenary; it was a shame to let it go by unnoticed.

XV

On Renan

THE OTHER DAY I HAD A PIECE OF RARE LEISURE AND WENT RIGHT THROUGH RENAN'S 'REMI-niscences of his youth.' I had not read the book for half a lifetime. When I had last seen it I was perhaps too young to weigh it as it should be weighed, but coming back to it after so many years, there returned to me with peculiar force the remark made to me by a Spaniard of profound scholarship and intelligence, 'To-day religion has no opponents worthy of it.'

I say that is a profound remark, and one which every modern man should meditate on, for it illustrates his time. I do not know whether it would be better for us or worse if there were now arrayed against the Christian religion men of the old stature, but at any rate it would be an intellectual pleasure to deal with them, and that intellectual pleasure is denied us.

If there was a man fitted to be a worthy opponent

of religion it was Renan, and take him all round he is the worthiest we have had within the last lifetime. He was a famous scholar, an admirable writer: his action was peculiarly forcible because he was trained for the Priesthood, and abandoned his vocation with an effect on his contemporaries comparable to the opposite effect of Newman's conversion in England a lifetime before. Renan puts forward his reasons with what seemed at that time—half a lifetime ago —so clear and cogent a process of thought that he was more responsible than any other man for the sceptical attitude towards Christian truth which prevailed in the last part of his own life. Yet on re-reading this famous and magnificently written piece of prose I was more and more impressed by its intellectual insufficiency.

I know it sounds bold to say this, but it is true. It is not only true that I feel this intellectual insufficiency in the man, but it is true that this intellectual insufficiency was there. Great as he is in scholarship, and much greater in the power of expression, in reasoning power he fails. Many people who read such lines from a pen such as mine, which does not pretend to scholarship, will think them insolent, but those who think so must remember that a truth worth telling is always either a well-worn thing, familiar to all, or a rare startling novelty, and this judgment of mine, though perhaps novel and startling and even, I am afraid to many people, offensive, is true. Renan lacked the intellectual capacity which an opponent of the Church should bring with him into controversy.

The lack of a sufficient intelligence in the discussion of any matter dependent upon the reason commonly shows itself in three ways:

First, by the taking for granted of postulates unexamined: accepted blindly as dogmas without being able to put forward the rational basis of acceptation.

Secondly, by not perceiving the implications of what one affirms to be true.

Thirdly, by not appreciating the extent of the field of discussion.

Now all those three insufficiencies are glaringly evident in Renan's work. He 'bolted whole,' as the phrase goes, sundry superficial judgments which he had read, but which he had not examined.

Next, he affirms things as though they were conclusively proved and certain, without perceiving the contradictions in which they involve him.

Lastly, he misses great areas of the field covered by the discussion upon which he is engaged.

I will give a few examples to establish this criticism. In a passage of the book where he is speaking of Scholasticism, he uses words which I translate almost textually, and which are to this effect, that he was trained as a young candidate for the Priesthood in the developed philosophy of the seventeenth-century theologians, and 'not in the puerile and barbaric scholasticism of the thirteenth century.'

Now that stamps the man at once. To begin with the thirteenth century is the century of St. Thomas. The words apply, and can only apply, to the gigantic and final intellectual work of St. Thomas. Renan admits that he has not read it, or, at any rate, that he had not read it when he abandoned his vocation and his Faith; yet he repeats with regard to it the ignorant, insufficient sentences copied from other men who were equally ignorant. He takes it for granted that something which he has never studied was of a particular character, and that this character is negligible, yet anyone who will spend even a few hours upon the most elementary of St. Thomas's work—say upon the first ten questions of the Summa—will see that those two particular adjectives 'puerile' and 'barbaric' are utterly inapplicable. Anyone is free to say that he differs from St. Thomas in his conclusions, that St. Thomas's reasoning is not convincing. Huxley, for instance, was certainly in that mood when he none the less bore witness to the towering intellectual power of the great Dominican doctor. But no one is free to say that the work is either puerile or barbaric. It is as though a man, having heard vaguely of Gothic architecture but never having seen a Gothic cathedral, having studied only the classical renaissance and the architecture of antiquity, were to say that the Gothic architecture in its highest moment (which by the way was contemporary with St. Thomas) was 'puny' and 'uncalculated.' Or it is as though a man unacquainted with Latin were to call Virgil 'prolix' and 'commonplace.'

And now for an example of Renan's lack of power to perceive the implications of his own statements. He rejects all the miraculous on the plea that a strict sequence of unalterable cause and effect governs the whole universe under an iron unity of law which can never be broken. Therefore the story that Our Lord stilled the tempest by supernatural power may be dismissed with contempt, for we know that every atmospheric movement is the necessary result of certain physical causes which are themselves the result of others, and so on, to the beginning of things— if, indeed, things ever had a beginning.

Renan was not the first man by many millions to say that, and will not be the last by many millions to say it, but he wholly missed the implication of it. The implication is that will is absent from the universe. When I lift up a fork with my hand from the table I am not interrupting the blind sequence of things, but am myself no more than part of this mechanical and material process. For if in any human action upon the universe around us we admit that Will is producing a disturbance, then necessarily and inevitably we must admit that superior Will could make a greater disturbance, and that a Supreme Will creative of the universe could exercise a special influence upon any scale it chose.

But Renan does not act either morally or intellectually upon the implications of his statement. He professes respect for truth, a duty to seek it and to promulgate it, indignation against falsehoods; in a word a moral scheme: but a moral scheme is incompatible with a merely mechanical universe.

Perhaps more striking than either of these first two intellectual faults is his third insufficiency, his inability to grasp the scale of the field in which he was conducting his discussion. He studies the Christian doctrines and the historical process whereby the Church came into being and developed. He studies on the same lines the affirmations of Scripture and especially of the Old Testament. He concludes that it is impossible after such study to believe what Christians believe, but he does not even attempt a survey of the positive grounds upon which they believe. He takes it for granted that there are no such grounds. His argument all through amounts to this: 'If only you knew what I know you would no longer hold your faith for an hour,' yet he had in front of him all the great body of Christian thought, ancient and modern, put forth by centuries of men who were at least his equals in his own department of philology, and his superiors in other departments of the inquiry. He does not meet, he seems actually not to know, the arguments which they have found sufficient; he leaves these arguments aside because (to be honest) he does not know that they exist.

Now a comparison of such insufficiencies points, I say, particularly to unintelligence; and I will conclude by what may seem a rather fantastic test of such unintelligence, but I think a sound one. Renan dates—the whole thing already sounds old-fashioned and outworn. He affected his own generation, but he does not continue to affect succeeding generations as the greater opponents of religion in the past still do, as for instance Voltaire still does, or Spinoza. I have chosen Renan as a particular instance, though his name is now growing unfamiliar to Englishmen, and though his original position is admittedly heavily lowered and is still falling.

I have chosen him because he was in his time the best example of that truth which I repeat, that the Faith has to-day no opponents worthy of itself. We may learn from the fate of Renan's work, I think, what the fate of other men's will be, men far less eloquent.

XVI

On Speeches

I READ IT ONCE IN A BOOK THAT SPEECH IS
WHAT DISTINGUISHES MAN FROM THE BRUTE
creation; but as I have recently learned from my
spiritual fathers in God that nothing whatever distinguishes man from the brute creation—not even
verse, let alone prayer—I think there must be some
mistake.

No matter. The point is that whether animals
speak or not (and I am sure that parrots do, for
I have heard them with my own ears), men speak.
But whereas speech may or may not distinguish man
from beasts (if, indeed, there be a distinction),
speeches—in the plural—do most undoubtedly distinguish politicians from ordinary vulgar people.

Now when I use this word 'politician,' let it not
be supposed that I am using it in a derogatory sense,
as though I were writing of parliamentarians alone,
or even lords. No. I mean any man who wants to
be a public futility; not only parliamentarians, but

town councillors, aldermen, secretaries of trades unions, and all that fauna which flourish under the still glories of peace. These, I say, are without a doubt to be distinguished from their fellow-men by the speechifying habit, which is not to be confused with the speechifying faculty.

The subject might be divided into a number of heads, like a hydra, but that would be cruelty. I prefer to treat it as a whole. Moreover, speeches themselves are divided into a number of heads, consciously or unconsciously, and it would be a great complication to extend the system to any discussion on speech in the abstract. There is a great tradition of a clergyman don at Oxford who, having married, and coming home with his wife from a long walk in the country, was heard saying: 'And seventeenthly, my dear. . . .' He was a modernist, and generally known to the younger men as The Hippopotamus.

If it be asked why your politically-minded man must be for ever making speeches (and these of inordinate length) the answer is, that only thus does he impress himself upon his fellow-beings. He cannot write (as a rule). He cannot think. He cannot model. He cannot paint. He cannot build. He cannot sail. (After all these clauses the words 'as a rule' should be introduced.) I will not say he cannot ride, because to the great comfort and well-being of this country an enormous number of public speakers can ride; many of them as cavalrymen, many of them as fox-hunters; and those who are one are usually the other. He cannot do any of the useful things (he certainly cannot dig); he cannot calculate, and he cannot—no, by God! he cannot—write verse. But any fool can speak.

Indeed, I heard of a man once who, having inherited a title, married an immensely wealthy heiress that had an iron spike in her left elbow. When he married her he could not put two words together; but she so trained him with this spike as she sat by his side at public functions, that he learned at last to make most fluent orations—especially about Peace among the Nations; and he would give illustrations of all concatenations which might interrupt international relations and lead to preparations for war-like operations to the great horror and protest of those who would suffer most heavily from the same.

All politically-minded men, I say, can speak. But this is mere tautology, because if politically-minded men could not speak they would not be politically-minded men, or, rather, they would not be known as politically-minded men. They might go on being politically-minded men till they were black in the face, like a friend of mine who always ardently desired to be a member of Parliament, and would, indeed, have become one, but that, though exceedingly fluent at home upon things of no consequence, such as proportional representation, he is dumb upon the platform, being struck with a sort of paralysis whenever he sees several hundred white blobs, called faces, arrayed before him like so many eggs: and I don't wonder.

I say that the speeches of the politician extend him in time and space. No politician would count if he made short speeches, or if he always made them in the same place. Therefore the politicians go all over the country. What do I say? All over Europe. Nay, more, all over the world—including the United States and the less Dutch parts of South Africa—swaying their arms, pointing their fingers, puffing out their chests and stomachs, and asserting that they are the last to deny.

Here the simple man will put a question: 'Pray, sir,' says he, 'if I design to be a politician, can you not tell me what least number of places I must visit, and what is the reasonably shortest time over which to extend one of my speeches?'

To him I shall answer: 'Little friend, you have misapprehended the complexity of your task. You have to consider not only the number of places you may visit, but their distance one from the other, and the coefficient of time in the matter, that is, over how many days you extend your speechifying. And as to the length of your speech, there, again, is a complexity. For it will depend upon the time in the evening and your own position; whether you are, for instance, the local member, or the mayor, or merely seconding an address, or proposing a vote of thanks: when the last train is, when the pubs shut, and so on.

But, roughly speaking, no man should speak even smoothly for less than half an hour, nor for more than one hour. If he speaks for less than half an hour he will very justly be called a very poor politician indeed. Whereas if he speaks for more than an hour, he may conceivably weary his audience. There is, of course, to this rule an exception, as to all rules. Thus I read of a Turkish politician recently who had spoken for six days—which beats the French Benches hollow; while there is, I am told, a man in Hanwell who speaks the whole time and all day long, and has done so for now fifteen years. But I am sure that he was never in the Government, for people with that facility of address are invariably shoved away on to the Back Benches of the Opposition before they retire from public life.

It was but the other day that a man sent me a letter asking me what matter one should put into a political speech. To which I answered, having an expert knowledge in this, that the whole art of a political speech is to put *nothing* into it. It is much more difficult than it sounds, and that is the answer to the puzzling question which so many have asked, and hitherto none have answered, 'Why does not everyone become a politician—seeing the money there is in it?'

Dear friends, believe me, to say absolutely nothing for a full hour is an art. I do not deny that the practice of a few years will make a man so expert in this subtle craft that he performs his task, as it were, unconsciously; on which account the phrase arose of Parliamentarians: 'They do it in their sleep.' But at the beginning it is very hard. Thus, a man speaking upon the matter of Germany and England in the old days before the War, would be naturally tempted to say something about blowing them out of the water, or (on the other side) of how they were our German cousins and how much he loved them, and how he hoped everybody else did, and how war between England and Germany was 'unthinkable.'

Digression: That horrible, barbarian word 'unthinkable' came into general use within my own lifetime. And I knew a jolly old squire ten miles off on the wrong side of the Downs, who used to think it was 'undrinkable'—and whenever he heard it in a speech would shout, ' 'Ear! 'Ear! 'Ear!' Thinking as he did so of the damnable dry wines which were coming in about the same time, to the exclusion of dark sherries, and of the pale tart brandy already ousting the black and sweet and soft brandy of his youth. End of digression.

But that would never do. The adept in the art would get up and say, 'We hear upon all sides that the Germans and ourselves, etc. etc.' (five minutes), 'but, my lords, ladies and gentlemen, it is easy to say these things. What are the facts?' (Here another ten minutes, introducing no facts.) 'My lords, ladies and gentlemen, he would, indeed, be a rash prophet who should pretend' (here another ten minutes in saying what the rash prophet would pretend).

'But it may be advanced—indeed, it has been advanced by my friend, the Secretary of State for Void' (here fifteen minutes, quite easy to fill up, because you may be perfectly certain that old Buggins has not advanced anything).

'What, then, is my conclusion?' (Here ten minutes, coming to no conclusion.)

When the adept has filled up his time thus, he

ends up with a peroration, and for that I will give you a tip. You cram it tight full of boasting, very much like the pumping of grease with a greasegun into a differential gear. You talk about the qualities of the race to which your audience belongs; you affirm your confidence in the future of their noble selves; and, in general, you let yourself go as no sycophant of any Oriental monarch ever let himself go in the worst phases of Asiatic corruption; and in this, after all, you do but show yourself a patriot.

It is also not a bad thing to conclude by saying that mere talking will do no good; that what we want is—and then you recite all the good qualities which you know the audience think they have.

Then you sit down.

I think I hear you asking me, 'What is it worth?'

Well, I have made a fair average computation, and I find it to be worth minus five hundred or six hundred a year, plus four hundred a year salary, and this for a space of anything between five and ten years. Then it becomes worth from eight hundred a year to twelve or fifteen hundred a year for five or six years, with a few chances of perquisites, but not many.

After that (*and here is the point*) speechifying suddenly becomes worth from five thousand to ten thousand a year and ample perquisites—opportunities of all kinds, in Promotions and Managing Directorships, and Lord knows what and all.

Take a fairly long lifetime of speechifying, from twenty-three years of age to seventy, and I should think little of a man who had not at the end of it left something over fifty thousand pounds, or who had not in the interval enjoyed an average income (counting everything) of well over three thousand pounds. It is not worth more than that: but it is worth that.

That is why people wonder at the absence of a general rush for public life, and the paucity of candidates. But courage! I think their numbers are about to increase.

XVII

On the Books That Change the World

THE OTHER DAY I WAS OCCUPYING MYSELF IN READING CALVIN'S "INSTITUTE" (WHICH YOU may also call, if you like, "Institutes"). I do not know whether many other people have acquainted themselves with this book. I had to turn to it in the course of my trade. It is not very interesting. But upon one thing everyone seems to be agreed, which is, that it was of sudden and vast effect.

Now, I could not help wondering as I read whether this universal verdict were exact. I do not say I have come to a conclusion on the matter, for I have not. I hold my judgment in suspense; yet I incline to ask more and more whether there were not other causes and effects between the publication of this book and the organisation everywhere, within ten years, of the solid structure combating the old religion and setting up in Europe a new kind of church with its own new organisation, its own new doctrine, discipline, and all the rest of it?

At first sight the question seems a foolish one.
There is no doubt that before the book appeared no
such organisation, no such body or church, was anywhere discoverable. There is no doubt that within a
few years of the book's appearance such a body was
discoverable spread everywhere throughout the
West, and giving that tone to the Reformation
which has lasted for nearly four hundred years.
Nor is there any doubt that you will find the main
lines, at least, of this great change set out in Calvin's
book. But I note that the effect is out of all proportion to the cause. It is this which makes me hesi-
tate. I can see no reason why any man reading the
Institute should suddenly be struck with fervour for
the new scheme, and I could not help wondering
whether there were not some common cause behind
the book and the political fact which followed.

It is an obvious truism that no book will be of
effect unless it finds a receptive medium. It would
be no good trying the *Pilgrim's Progress* on in
County Clare, nor would the 'Pleasant Sunday Afternoon Association' have much truck with *Corneille*.
If that book which put most clearly what it wanted
to say, and was followed by a most prodigious sequel
and seeming consequence (I mean Rousseau's *Contrat Social*) had had no one to appeal to but an audi-

ence of retired professional politicians, all rich, they might have got fun out of it, but certainly not conviction. Rousseau's *Contrat Social* fell on soil exactly suited to it—and so it was with Calvin's *Institute*. There was lying ready for Calvin's book a fervent mass of protest, which wanted to be told of some way out, whereby they could get rid of the priest without destroying society. But why *that* way out? And how can we believe that the mere statement in the book of a certain scheme of things, put without fire, lucid, but lacking enthusiasm, suddenly created the frenzied cavalry charges of the religious wars, the enthusiasts on the Scotch hills, and the formidable vision of Geneva?

It may also be argued that these books which look as though they change the world are themselves much more effects than causes. Indeed, we know that many of these great changes have come with no book at all to herald them, though few have come without some book to summarize them sooner or later. It would seem as though the great movements of history arose like those sudden broad waves heaving out of the deep sea in calm weather, and rolling forth incomprehensibly under no wind. The emotion once produced may or may not make a book, may or may not create an organism. But can we give to these most famous books, these books which are immediately followed by tremendous things, the name of causes? Are those men justified who regret that they were born too late to have written the Koran? Or, again, would it have been enough to write the book? Is it that the genius of a man shining through the book coincides with a great happening in the mind of man, so that the author, of whatever genius, is but the instrument of this mood?

And, by the way, the Koran, read in a translation, is sometimes incomprehensible and always poor. Will not some one of the many English scholars who are steeped in Arabic explain to us why it is of such effect in its original?

Supposing this doubt to be resolved in the affirmative: supposing we were to come to the conclusion that the book did not, indeed, produce the thing, and that the mighty effects of Calvinism, of the Republic, of modern Collectivism, did not spring from the *Institute*, from the *Contrat*, from that abominably boring, endless haystack, Marx's *Kapital*? Are we, then, to conclude that no books are of such effect? Must we condemn to despair those thousands of young ambitious men dying to change the world by the typewritten word, and those myriads and myriads of rather more elderly women engaged in the same task? God forbid!

There is, I fancy, a kind of book which certainly influences the world directly, and, it may be truly said, is an original cause to the effect it creates. It is not the book which merely expresses what its audience was already feeling in a confused fashion, nor the book which fires enthusiasm by rhetoric; but the book which tells clearly the discovery of some truth, giving positive evidence for the same.

That, as it seems to me, is quite certainly a point of departure; of such books you can say, 'This made all the difference'—when you find them! But remember that the greater part of them remain unknown. There are some very famous, of which the most famous, and the most deservedly famous, is Descartes's *Discourse on Method*. There is the *Principia* of Newton. But I believe there to be a great number which have no such effect and remain known to but a few. I notice sometimes, in the life around me, that men begin talking more and more in terms of this or that, which had been unfamiliar to them thirty years ago, and that the way in which they handle the thing distinctly points to some obscure book written for a few hundred readers, most of whom will forget where they read it, and many of whom are soon convinced that the ideas were original to themselves.

Of what book, for instance, can you say that it was the origin in the modern world of our present attitude towards physical science? (By which phrase I do not mean our present attitude towards the body of ascertained and proved facts of physical science, but our attitude towards that old-fashioned mode of thought which we associate with the now discredited word 'scientist.') Will you find me the book which started the ball rolling of that mood? To-day a curious smile lights up the face of ironic men when they hear such words as 'ether,' or still worse, 'the crust of the earth.' (Here I must admit in fairness that the latter is only a survival: still, even I can remember the time when the Molten Interior, with a thin crust outside, was dogma.) Or, again, who started that revival of Thomism which, though it has had no effect here as yet, is so increasingly marked upon the continent of Europe? There have been many books on that line. I doubt if you will find one which you can point to as the origin.

In this same connexion let me conclude with a consoling thought. The epoch-making works of our own time are worth nothing. Is it not a pure joy to remember this? Every year for twenty years past or more there has appeared at least one book, and usually half a dozen, announced not only by their publishers and through advertisement, nor only by the poor devils of reviewers, as changing the whole spirit of man: upon War, upon Theology, upon History. Their fame lasts, when they are very great, for three months; when they are of a lesser rank, for ten days. And the modern world goes on its bumping run downhill. Nor do any of these books have any enduring effect.

Lord! What a regiment we have had of them! The book before the War to show that modern war was impossible, because it would cost so much; the book after the War that showed how paying enormous tribute to a foreign nation ruined that nation and enriched yourself; the book showing that you couldn't fly through the air; that, if you did, it was a waste of time; the book showing that flying through the air was the key to all victory, wealth, happiness and repose; the book showing that fleets could never hold the narrow seas; the book showing that they were more triumphant than ever in the narrow seas; the book opening the glorious future of man; the book which showed clearly that the world had long ago cut its own throat.

127

And my delight is that they are still going on! Why, it was only this morning that I came across yet another book; this time upon the revelations of the Great Pyramid and upon the end of world. The world is to end next summer. I don't believe it. It is too good to be true.

XVIII

On Gibbon

GIBBON'S "DECLINE AND FALL" IS AN EXAMPLE OF THE TRUTH THAT 'A WRITER'S BUSINESS is to write.' I do not know if Aristotle said this. If he did not, he ought to have. The writer, as writer, is there to write stuff which the reader, as reader, will like to read. If he does that, he has fulfilled his being—as a writer. Whether he has fulfilled his being in other ways is his own lookout. Though, mind you, a lot depends on it!

Hence the big quarrel (which has not yet begun) between Gibbon as a writer and Gibbon as an historian. Sooner or later people will discover—it is only a question of starting the ball rolling—that Gibbon had little historical sense, and, on the top of that, did not wish to tell the truth, but rather to attack. On which account he is a bad historian. But as a writer—what a writer!

I have not read all the books in the English language, but of such as I have read, Gibbon's *De-*

129

cline and Fall is far and away the most readable. I speak not only for myself, but I believe for hundreds of others, over a period which will soon cover a century and a half, when I say that you can pick him up at any moment, open him where you will, read him for ten minutes or half an hour or half a day, and lay him down delighted. I verily believe there is not a dull line in the enormous work. Certainly there is not a dull page. For wit, for concision, for exactitude of expression, for *meat* (the right word), I know not his equal.

It has been said that literary work is bad when you can parody it; by which is meant, I suppose, that such work must have been stretched on a stiff framework, lacking vitality. That may be true of verse that is easy to parody, though I doubt it. It is certainly not true of prose. To parody Gibbon is the easiest thing in the world, and it has been done with success dozens of times—notably in the famous imaginary passage concerning the Barbarian Queen and the Roman Senate. But, then, so is the style of the Jacobean Old Testament easily patient of parody; so is Johnson's glorious *Rasselas;* so are any number of others. The truth would seem to be that you can parody whatever has strong rhythmic flow and a clearly apparent, outstanding method.

But what you cannot parody in Gibbon is the stuff itself. By this I mean that if you sat down to write a page of contemporary history in the manner of Gibbon, you would fail to touch the mark. You could parody a sentence, but you could not achieve in a long passage the full manner. (The same, by the way, is true of Shakespeare's blank verse.)

Thus clever men have hit off a page or two that looks like Tacitus, but never a man has written a page of Tacitus; and those who think that many pages of Tacitus were forged by moderns, lay themselves under a heavy condemnation.

Gibbon can be parodied because he constructed for himself an admirable vehicle. He designed that channel through which his thought should flow. How successfully he designed it we may discover from this very interesting and (I think) little-known example: That Lingard, when he sat down to lay the foundations of modern English history—(he was the first man to build it up on the careful consultation of original documents—he was the first expert: before him all were amateurs: he is the quarry to which all after him turned for their references)—was, in the matter of mere style, forced into the model of Gibbon. The writing of Lingard, thus founding all modern English history, is dull. The writing of Gibbon is brilliant. But Lingard's style was made by Gibbon all the same.

Gibbon fashioned a vehicle wherein could repose in the least space, and yet with the greatest lucidity, all the fact (or fiction) which he desired to present. In these antitheses of his the adjective, the adverb, the verb, the noun, each tell you what he desired to tell. There is nothing redundant to fog the mind; there is nothing omitted to confuse it. The order also is perfect; and the whole has the supreme quality of good work, which is that it marches directly towards its end and attains it.

I have said that Gibbon's *Decline and Fall* may be picked up anywhere at any hour and read with pleasure: with satisfaction: for any space of time, short or long. But there is more than that. One can take it up at almost any period of one's life and so delight in it. To speak for myself alone, I have read it in this fashion for thirty-five years. And there is more still. You can go back to him as often as you like. That is surely the supreme test! You can (at least, I can) read the very same passage over and over again, each time within a few days of the last, and suffer no fatigue, any more than one may suffer fatigue from the prospect of a familiar but satisfying landscape.

He has been blamed for a lack of proportion, devoting, as he does, great space to the earlier development of his theme, condensing, as he does, its later phases. This seems to me a false criticism—though he himself may have inclined to it. His business was to discover a certain process comparable (in his mind) to the ruin of a building: to wit, the disintegration of the old pagan and Roman and Greek culture and the disassociation of its elements into the Dark and Middle Ages. It was right (with this thesis in his mind) to dwell upon the main and earlier part of the disintegration, to condense the story of what he thought to be the final collapse. Perhaps he grew hurried at the end: but the result is good. The ruin of a thing is interesting in proportion as somewhat of that thing remains. It loses interest in proportion as the structure loses its original form, and after Charlemagne all the Occident is transformed.

But I have said that Gibbon was unhistorical: that he lacked historical sense, and even that he lied. Now here I know that the most of my readers will strongly disagree with me. I will attempt to defend that position, for I am convinced of its truth.

It is a double position: I say in the first place that Gibbon lacked the historic sense. I say in the second place that he lied. How can such enormities be held?

As to the first. It seems to me that he lacked the historic sense quite as much as—much more than—Pope lacked the granite quality of Homer. When Homer (or the Ballad-club or Committee, or what you will) wrote:

Ὣς οἱ μὲν μάρναντο δέμας πυρὸς αἰθομένοιο,

he (or they) carved in stone. When Pope wrote:

'So like a raging fire that the combat burns,

And now it rises, now it sinks, by turns. . . .'

(I quote only from memory), he was not chiselling upon a hard surface, he was building up a mosaic. He was not doing bad stuff. He was a great poet. The second line is a just illumination of the first. But it is not Homer (excuse me, the Committee). The whole point of Homer is knocking one down with a verb and a noun and a conventional adjective. How it is done nobody knows. It is done in the New Testament: *'Confidite, Ego Vici Mundum.'* It is done in the song of Roland: 'To God on His Holy Hill in the City of Paradise.' It is done in the Border Ballads over and over again. It is done in the twelfth century, Angevin French singing the burial of Iseult: 'She by him and he by her.' How it is done nobody knows. If anyone could know, anyone could be a poet. But I perceive that, as usual, I am digressing and following a second hare. To return to Gibbon.

He lacked the historic sense. History (let me say it for the fortieth time in quotation of Michelet) should be a resurrection of the flesh. You cannot write history unless you can get into the very skin of the past. A historian is here something of what an actor is. Thus does he put life into dead things.

Now Gibbon never attempted this. He did not feel as the first ages of the Empire felt, for he made them more rationalist, less transcendental than they were; he could not appreciate their growing sense of Unseen Things, nor their inheritance from ancient mysteries. Therefore when he gets to the Christian centuries he is unhistorical. He does not convey to his reader why or how men thought it of such awful import to discover what their pagan predecessors would have called 'The nature of the gods.' He merely jokes about it. That (with deference to so great a genius) is childish. It is not explaining a past epoch to laugh at what you do not understand, any more than it is explaining a foreign country to jeer at it and say, 'Look at those absurd foreigners!'

It is of supreme interest to our civilisation that

it should understand *why* the theological debate from Arianism to the Iconoclasts arose, and of what critical importance it was to the future of our race. Yet in this even the *Cambridge History* has more historic sense than Gibbon. The *Cambridge History* at least tells its readers what might have happened to Europe had Arianism won. But Gibbon has no conception of that battle's position in the making of Europe.

Am I right also in saying that he lied? Yes, I think I am; though the word is a strong one. He so hated the Christian religion that he did, not once, but a hundred times, suppress essential facts, wilfully distorting and wilfully over-emphasising. It is true that he may be excused on the plea that he did not burrow into original authorities, but wrote in a secondary fashion, working up the more laborious Frenchmen (and here and there, in translations, a German) of his time. This can be proved from his use of references. Where his Continental authorities go wrong, he goes wrong. He rarely follows up the original quotation.

Further, he often and deliberately distorted what he knew to be historical facts. He deliberately omitted things he must have known, and deliberately over-emphasised things that he could not but have discovered to be unimportant. He talks (*after* the publication of the full eighteenth-century work on the Catacombs) inexcusable nonsense about the use of images in the early Church. In the matter of the True Cross, the First Council of Ephesus, and perhaps another dozen capital examples, he plays the part of a mere advocate, and a most alien advocate at that.

Hence it is that anyone with sufficient leisure and industry may easily riddle him as a historian. The task has not yet been accomplished, but it lies ready for anyone who chooses to undertake it.

But as a writer, as a glory to the Letters of England, he is unassailable.

XIX

On Translation

I HAVE OFTEN WRITTEN ON TRANSLATION. LET ME WRITE OF IT AGAIN, FOR IT IS OF HIGH political importance. For the time in which we live has a particular need for true translation: that is, for the full rendering into one tongue of what has appeared in another; for a rendering inspired with the original spirit. The reason that is so is that Christendom happens to have fallen into a state the like of which has, I think, no parallel in history. It has become a culture, essentially one in what it desires to express: violently divided in its instruments of expression, with vast and innumerable opportunities for *false* communications.

We, of Europe, are a closely united civilisation which might also be called a 'paradoxically' united civilisation, considering those elements of diversity which I am about to consider. Our unity of conception, our unity of script (which is but a material thing), much more our unity of habitual life (our furniture, our communion in all that escapes language, music and the pictorial arts, and, indeed, in spite of the tremendous schism, our remembered unity of religion), face throughout the Occident no less than five quite separate major idioms, which five major idioms have attached to them at least one hundred minor ones. No man, not the most cultured and travelled man, possesses fully these five idioms. A very few men may claim to three; a few thousand (out of many millions) to two.

It is customary to compare the various States of modern Western Europe to the States of ancient Greece. 'There,' we are told, 'you also had high local patriotism, with its necessary corollary of inter-state wars; there you had the sentiment of unity side by side with the sentiment of high differentiation.' Innumerable parallels are drawn between Sparta, Athens, Corinth and the modern European States; modern men are flattered by a comparison between themselves and any one of these antiquities. But on the test of familiar language the whole thing breaks down. Anyone could have walked from the Gulf under Olympus to the Cape southernmost of the Peloponnesus and everywhere spoken his own tongue. It was a language differentiated indeed, but more of one kind than the languages of the Northumberland and the Sussex peasant to-day, let alone the languages of Dover and Calais, Milan and Zurich, Udine and Zaghreb. A cultivated man of fourth-century Hellas had one national literature passionately loved, and everywhere fully adapted to his mind, both in its archaic and in its contemporary form. But to-day the well-born and well-to-do man, English, French, Italian, Castilian, German, must laboriously learn one or all of the other four idioms, to be able to test European literature at all.

I, for instance, who am writing this, can make my way with difficulty through an Italian or Spanish newspaper. I cannot do this with a German newspaper. I can read a French newspaper not, well, as though it were English, but still with a fairly full comprehension. When it comes to the literature of these countries, say the ordinary novel, I cannot read German at all, nor, with any ease Italian, nor, save at three-quarters guess-work, the Castilian; when it comes to great literature, and an immediate feeling of excellence through reading, I am no use at all, except in English. Though I have a wide current acquaintance with French I could never be sure of my judgment as to a French piece of verse, still less as to French prose. In my acquaintance I count highly-cultivated men—perhaps a dozen of them—with a full judgment of two or even three idioms foreign to my own; but I have, in the whole course of a life which has brought me up against a great many other men, only known two who were even generally acquainted with the five idioms; not one who was at home in all.

So here we are, all of one western world, dressing and living much alike, and all pouring out a mass of ideas perpetually, yet chained to languages in five great groups, separated each from the others as never were the idioms of any united civilisation before. Let us get that idea very fully into our minds, for it is the foundation of all that can now be said with regard to the insistent necessity of good translation.

It is always valuable to emphasise the truth by the use of contrast. If anyone fail to appreciate how singular is our present state of affairs in Europe, let him consider any known phase of the past. The past had always one, or at the most two, great literary idioms. Either a civilisation had one idiom, as had early Greece, and (it may be assumed) the Assyrian and Egyptian civilisations, or it had, as had the great society from which we all spring, the Greco-Roman Empire, two combined. Now one idiom needs no discussion. With all its differentiation into dialects and slang, and false accent, and the rest, one idiom is a known thing. English to-day is English, and anyone of sufficient taste, being born an Englishman, or an English-speaking man, can read what is written in that medium and judge it; and anyone, whether of taste or not, can understand what is said or written in that medium. Such has been the position of mankind normally with regard to 'The Semantic' (to quote the expression created by the great Jewish writer, Michel Bréal) throughout the history of mankind. In the five formative centuries of our Western culture, the centuries of the Conversion and of the founding of Christendom, two main idioms stood side by side, the Greek and the Latin. It was not abnormal for the educated man of that ancient society, the cultured minority on which tradition always hangs, to be equally familiar with both. The civilisation of antiquity from the fall of Corinth to well into the fourth century was bilingual. A Roman gentleman under the Antonines could express exactly the same shade of thought indifferently in Greek or in Latin, as we can indifferently by the pen or the typewriter.

There was a later moment in which it looked as though modern Europe would have a similar happy fate, and the French and the English idioms would become between them the combined method of all cultivated expression. Gibbon originally intended French to be the medium of his history. Napoleon and the French Armies, attempting to achieve European unity, produced its opposite. They aroused national teaching, destroyed the universal use of French, and the isolated idiomatic groups have come to stay for some few generations at least. Before the French Revolution every English gentleman who counted was supposed to speak French correctly. After Waterloo it was not well-bred to speak French without an accent.

It is not possible for any large body of men to grasp even the five idioms, let alone their derivatives; and as for those, very few men can boast even a rough acquaintance with French, English, German, Italian and Spanish, their influence is not sufficient to form a flux. Yet, at the same time, a common commercial life has bred a most abominable facility in false mechanical translation. Anyone can, for a few pence, buy a thoroughly false translation of a thousand English words into much the same number of Spanish, done in an hour. Therefore is the necessity for good translation urgent, lest vile 'translation Bureaus'—worthy children of Big Business—should become universal.

It would not be difficult to throw this thesis into a negative form.

We all know what happens to each idiom when it is left uninspired by the knowledge of the others. Those very insufficient people who imagine for the moment that English (for instance) will become a universal medium for the white civilisation, must admit that its wide spreading has had the most lamentable effects upon its quality. Those insanely proud men who thought that the official German might so spread should know that, if it had so spread, our thought would have perished. Those punctilious and exact men who refer everything to their native French have long ago discovered that their instrument worked in too narrow a field. We must have, for the survival and health of the Occident, good translation. We have not got it.

Now, let us examine the conditions under which it can be obtained, the enemies of its erection, the qualities properly attaching to it. Good translation must be founded upon a knowledge of the medium *into which* some foreign matter is to be rendered. Let us set that down for a canon of this novel but necessary science. To translate German into English you need an English mind; to translate French into Spanish you need a Spanish mind—and so forth.

144

Nothing worth doing will ever be done the other way about. There is no one so familiar with an idiom foreign to his own that he can be certain of imparting to that foreign idiom a native tone. Our minds are so made that they can appreciate far more readily than they can express. We can know a voice to its inmost, yet mimic it ill. I can make out of 'Carlon li re e toz sa baronie,' 'Charles the King and his Barony'—a translation which (I boast) has the call of the original. But I cannot put into early French 'revisit the glimpses of the moon.'

It is, indeed, essential that a translator should have, if not a minute and detailed knowledge of that idiom out of which he translates, yet, at any rate, an enthusiastic sympathy with its spirit; but more essential still is his unusually perfect handling of his own tongue.

The second canon would seem to be this: that the soul of the original should re-arise in the translation. Now here we have a very pretty discussion. First let us note that some of the very best translators in the world have been admittedly literal; that is, they have been translators professionally engaged in not missing one word of the original. The monumental example of this is St. Jerome's rendering of the Hebrew Scriptures into Latin, and the great derivative of that enormous feat, the translation of the Old Testament into English, even then archaic, under James I of England. In this case, from the very nature of the task, the translator was not concerned with literary effect, but with a much more important thing, exactitude of message. He was not like a man translating Homer; he was like a man decoding a foreign telegram in time of war, upon the precise value of each word in which turn facts vastly important to him.

Yet these two great literal efforts, the Latin Vulgate and the Jacobean English Bible, are manifestly successful. Here, then, is a paradox! How was that success achieved? I take it that the success was achieved by the intensity of emotion involved. A man having to translate words which mean in their original exactly this, and nothing but this, 'Israel coming out of Egypt, the House of Jacob out of a barbarous people,' made of it the splendid trumpet entry of the Vesper psalm *in Exitu*. A man having to translate 'The stars which rise just before the sun made a loud chorus, and the elementals directly produced by the Creator did the same in their happiness,' produced, 'When the morning stars sang together, and the sons of God shouted for joy.'

146

If we were to aim at good translation by this literal method, uninjured by enthusiasm, we should fail. It is a happy indirect result, appearing under very exceptional circumstances apart from the will. There can be no consciously good translations of the kind. For instance (to take a province with which I am most familiar), the finest pieces of modern French rhetoric have occasionally been reproduced in the English Press, those of Jaurès, for instance. The translator translated literally, and the result is monkey-talk.

Good translation must (unless a white heat of enthusiasm is present as a solvent) consciously attempt the spirit of the original at the expense of the letter. Now this is much the same as saying that the translator must be of original talent; he must himself create; he must have power of his own. A translated work must, to be excellent, normally be the product of an exceptional writer. It is true, indeed, that the good translator is very often no first-rate creator outside the field of translation. I will quote four examples of this: Bédier's translation of the *Tristan et Iseult,* out of the old French into modern, which is one of the great books of our generation; Urquhart's translation of the first books of Rabelais, which is incomparably good;

Dasent's *Tales from the Norse;* and Church's *Stories from Homer.* None of these four men did anything outside translation to be compared with their triumphs as translators. But, at any rate, their quality lies in the fact that they transposed, not copied, their originals. They did what the great painter does when he transfers the thing seen to other seers. They did what a great actor does when he introduces a past mind through his own mind to the mind of his audience.

We conclude, then, that great translation needs exceptional talent, desiring to reproduce, and able to reproduce, the spirtual rhythm, the character, the essence of the original thing.

Now let us consider the enemies of such artistic effort; for if we consider these, we shall understand why that effort fails us to-day—especially in England. England to-day is more cut off from the power of Europe than ever she has been before; and bad translation is one great factor in that misfortune of sterilisation, ignorance and ineptitude.

The prime enemy of good translation is the woeful error that translation is a mechanical affair. It is an error founded upon the universal error of the generation just past, the time out of which we are now emerging, that all is measurable and calculable; that the mechanical outweighs the organic; that the quantitative is alone considerable, and that wisdom speaks in terms of numbers alone (divorced from their mystical quality). It even tries to reduce music and colour to the mathematic. At bottom it is the Pythagorean error robbed of the Pythagorean vision.

To come down to earth again, this error in the matter of translation is the conception that words are mere dead symbols, one in one language exactly corresponding to one in another.

> *Fluminaque antiquos subterlabentia muros.*
> 'Rivers also running under old walls.'

or again:

> *Il monta dans sa gloire, et son Aigle mourut.*
> 'He rose in his glory and his Eagle died.'

or again:

> *Sant Iago, y Sierra l'Espagna!*
> 'St. James: and close up the ranks, Spain.'

or again:

> Τῷ δ᾽ ἅμα τεσσαράκουτα μέλαιναι νῆες ἐπουτο.
> 'He was followed by forty black ships.'

If you go on translating like that no wonder you also get the newspaper translation as all-sufficient to-day; and the appalling misinterpretation of national feelings abroad which is a curse of our modern Press.

A natural consequence of this great fundamental error is the conception that translation can be bought and sold at a minimum price. It is true that the heaven-born translator, like the heaven-born poet, can be bought cheap sometimes and starved to death. But the idea that good translation—indeed, the only translation worth having at all—is available as a marketable commodity in great quantities with a price attached to it, follows directly upon the folly and baseness of modern commerce.

Somebody says, 'Let us publish an English translation of Anatole France,' and they think that anyone will do as translator so long as he knows that *vache* means a cow and *maison* a house. They do not exactly seek the cheapest workmen, but they take it for granted that there is a great company of people able to translate high French prose into English, any one of whom is pretty well as good as another. It won't do. The end of that commercial method is an extending ignorance of each idiom with regard to the rest. It emphasizes our differences.

I have before me an excellent instance of this kind of thing. The French politician called Viviani wrote after 1918 an account, very accurate and important as a political document, not very remarkable in style, of the origins of the Great War. He exactly noted the hours and dates of the critical days, July 26th-August 4th, 1914, and described minutely and conclusively the interchange of documents and messages between Berlin, Vienna and St. Petersburg. This absolutely essential and capital contribution to European history, establishing the guilt of the Prussian general staff, was translated into an English which it is impossible to qualify in decent language. The execrable hotch-potch produced was submitted to the English Press for review. What happened was inevitable. The pro-French papers in England said it was a very fine book, but made it look ridiculous when they quoted even a phrase. The pro-German papers quoted the same phrases as comic absurdities. Meanwhile, the English educated public remained quite ignorant of a discussion which is vital to the comprehension of international politics to-day.

Here it may be objected that translation such as I advocate must be capricious; that only rare and spontaneous effort could produce it; that nothing universal of the sort could be expected; that it could only be accidental—like good verse.

This would be a sound objection as applied to the first-rate, the astonishing translation. But there seems to me to lie between it and the commercial rubbish of our time a large middle zone unfilled. Only here and there, as exceptions, do you find great passages of prose; but that is no reason why we should write like the Parliamentarians or their supporters in the popular papers. Only here and there do you find remarkable wine; but that is no reason why one should put up with vinegar. Of translation it must be said as of prose and of wine, that (unlike affection, verse and sacrifice) its core is sound mediocrity; a daily level beneath which it should not sink. Now beneath that daily level it has lately —for some thirty years—sunk very damnably in England.

What economic basis is there for its recovery? To that question, as to parallel questions in twenty other matters, there are only two answers, demand or endowment. Either there must be a demand for good translations sufficient to pay for the same, or rich men (or the poor old State, or other corporations) must endow. The latter suggestion is not so fantastic as it sounds. A great Jewish fortune has been employed most genuinely and usefully already in this field: I refer to the Loeb series. It is not, then, impossible to hope that a price could be paid to-day for good translations from contemporary Continental work. But, at any rate, something must be done to get over the present famine, or England will lose her European culture.

The converse is, happily, not to be feared. English work is well translated abroad. But the European work of the Continent is hardly known in England, with the result that an exceedingly alien, distorting pressure is received from America (and a little from the Colonies) and nothing set up to preserve tradition. We have already seen the effect of this upon our daily Press. It is invading our literature as well. Another generation of it and English letters will lose their anchor-hold in Christendom, and go adrift.

We must have some machinery whereby good translation of worthy material is paid the same rates as is that much easier effort, plain writing. If we don't get it *our* future suffers, and irretrievably.

*   *   *   *   *

But the difficulties are formidable, and traps have been spotted long ago.

153

I have not myself done much translation in my time, but the little I have done has caused me painful labour, and at the price of that labour I think I can claim to know something about it. I have translated from French, which I know well, but by no means perfectly, into English, which I have at my command. In particular, I have translated one of the best pieces of prose in our time—already mentioned in this—M. Bédier's compilation of the Tristan legends. But when I look back upon my own work in translation and ask myself why this passage is more successful than that passage, I find the question very difficult to answer.

The main obvious points are the lack of exact correspondence between individual words in two different languages, the different trick of thought in two civilisations (by which what is rhetorical in the one, for instance, may seem plain prose in the other, or by which the order of thought in the one turns chaotic in the other), conceptions in the one not occurring at all in the other (for instance, the French words *constater, droit, directive*; the English words *gentleman, scholar, fun*), and so forth. But this is only the very beginning of the business.

There is rhythm. There is euphony. There is the atmosphere which words build up round them-

selves and which depend upon a thousand little social influences and traditions, familiar to their habitat,
alien and blankly unknown elsewhere.

There is sometimes an extreme difficulty in rendering a perfectly straightforward statement; as, for
instance, the French military verb *flotter*. When
you say that a line '*flottait*,' or when you apply the
metaphor in argument, or any other form of con-
test, you mean a state of affairs exceedingly difficult
to translate into English, though it is a perfectly
definite statement of events and has a very precise
meaning. You cannot render it 'the line was breaking' or 'the line was beginning to break.' 'The line
was in danger of breaking' is quite another set of
ideas. It does not exactly mean 'the line was weak-
ening.' I suppose the only approximate rendering
would be reached through a great expansion into
English words thus: 'The line was growing somewhat uncertain, it was already sinuous, and was in a
condition which might lead to wavering and possibly even to breaking, were the movement continued.' It means all that. Or rather, it means that
restricted, that exact, thing.

Then there is the series of gradations in the
emphasis with which statements are made. They
come, as it were, in different sized steps, according

to the language. In one language there will be
five or six steps between the same two extremes,
in another only a couple, in another fifty. Hardly
ever will the edges of any two correspond.

And if this is true of straightforward statements
it is much more true of what colours every sentence in prose—mood. If you do not translate a
dignified sentence by another dignified sentence it
is no translation at all. If you do not render some
proportion of irony in the original by a similar
proportion of irony in the version, it is no translation
either. If you substitute petulance for indignation,
or a snigger for a sneer, or a piece of violence for a
weighty and considered blow, you have missed your
point.

The extreme difficulty of translation, its extreme
subtlety, its artistic quality, is seen also in this: that
the great prose effects which have vitally moved one
civilisation are nearly always unknown to another;
and this is not only through the imperfection of
language, but through the sheer impossibility of
rendering the full effect of the original, save by
some piece of luck or some stroke of genius. An
example is Rousseau's *Social Contract*. Of the very
few scholarly men who have dealt with the subject
of the French Revolution in England, not one un-

derstands why Rousseau's *Social Contract* had its enormous effect. As certainly no Frenchman I ever met had the least conception of the effect the Book of Common Prayer has upon an English reader.

Nevertheless, genius sometimes does the trick. One would say that Le Sage could not be translated—at least, not so as to give the full pleasure of the original, and yet I have in my house, and constantly re-read, the English translation (by Joseph Thomas, 1841) of the *Asmodeus*. It is perfect. It is, so to speak, Le Sage come to life again in an English dress. But I do not know if it has been done for his *Gil Blas*.

Angelier did it for Robert Burns, and I know at least two passages, one in *Julius Cæsar* and the other in *Romeo and Juliet*, which have been exactly hit off in French; but the thing is as rare as can be.

Not an essential to true translation, but a wonderful aid to it, is the intimate knowledge of daily life among the people *from* whose language you translate. In reading the other day a book of Mrs. Wharton's on the French, I got that feeling of intimacy, and I think *The Silence of Colonel Bramble* by a French-speaking Jew has something of the same sort of intimacy with the English mind. Mrs. Wharton's recent book had nothing to do with translation; it was a mere appreciation of the French, and it was astonishingly well done, while *The Silence of Colonel Bramble* professes to be no more than fiction. But they both illustrate the spirit I mean. It is not exactly sympathy with the foreign mind; it is a penetration of it.

Mere ignorance accounts for a good deal of bad translation; much more than one might imagine. Talking of Rousseau's *Social Contract*, I remember how at Oxford a Don, exposing to me the errors of that immortal booklet, showed me in some work (one of Maine's, perhaps) an extraordinary blunder which he did not know was a blunder. The authority he quoted to me had translated Rousseau's phrase: 'The general will is always direct' (*droite*), by the absurd: 'The general will is always right.' And the solemn gentleman had gone on to argue very painfully that Rousseau had made a mistake, that the general will was not always right—about Titus Oates, for instance; or Boers during the South African War; or anything else you like.

One of the most difficult problems of all those which meet one in translation is the problem of rendering conventional exaggeration. There is nothing commoner in French political writing and speaking than putting, in the present tense and in an absolute manner, a catastrophe against which the author only intends to warn you, and which may not even be probable. Not a year ago a prominent French parliamentarian said in a speech upon the Budget (which was literally translated into the English papers) words which, if exactly rendered, would run somewhat as follows: 'You have led our unfortunate people to complete ruin.' The real translation would be in English: 'I agree with the honourable gentleman when he says that we shall certainly pull through; but, meanwhile, there is urgent necessity for retrenchment, etc.'—a form of words equally false, literally. The one says more, the other less, than the bald truth. This form of over-emphasis is in the genius of the French language. You find it as far back as the *Song of Roland*. All languages have their form of exaggerated statement, to be taken in a spirit quite different from the literal. But the users of each language are aware of the convention. The foreigner is not. When a Frenchman says of a hedging politician that he is a traitor, and an Englishman that he yields to no one in his admiration for his opponent's spotless integrity, they neither of them mean to be taken literally. Each means that the fellow is something of a dirty dog in his public capacity, but no doubt decent enough in his mediocre private life.

Here is another pitfall: the overlapping of words. The same word is not only used in many different senses in every language, but in every language any one word you may take performs several tasks. When you render it into another language by what you believe to be its equivalent, you are picking up a different instrument. You are setting to work a different machine which does *some* work similar to the word you are translating, but also does *other* work the translated word cannot touch.

Take, for instance, the word *street*, and the French word *rue*. There are some exceedingly exiguous and dry statements in which—short of the fact that the mental picture called up is different in the two cases—the one word is a translation of the other. But each word connotes in each language a set of uses only some of which are common to both languages. Notably in this case '*rue*' vaguely suggests, the moment you use it, the memory of street fighting in revolution and civil war. To the English mind 'street' suggests the general and commonplace. Behind the one is the atmosphere of '*descendre dans la rue*,' which has been used for generations in French to mean armed revolt against existing authority; in the other there is the atmosphere of 'man in the street' and all the civilian domestic associations of the word *street* in the English language.

The Gallic word *cheval* (which the Latins adopted) hangs on to a whole crowd of images— the Dark and the Middle Ages, the hierarchy of feudal society, generosity: it stands for knighthood, 'chevalier,' and 'chivalry.' The word *horse* does nothing of the kind. It is bound up with a whole group of other associations, various amusements, especially, and also grotesquely enough with the idea of solidity or largeness. A good horseman is not a knight. Horsemanship is not chivalric. Horse-sense and a horse-face have nothing of 'cheval' about them. A horsey man is no Bayard. The early French line on the Holy Land *'la doit on faire chevalerie'* still means *'there must one go riding horses.'* But it connotes a Crusade. You cannot translate that phrase by any English word based on the word *horse*. To take a converse instance: you cannot get a modern French synonym for the English word *school* in the sense of *public school* with its profound social meaning; and this word suggests another obvious trap in translation. The same word will be used in a language for two very different images which have yet something fundamentally in common. To give even a faint hint of what an Englishman means when he says of two Etonians: 'They were at the same school,' you must use the French word *collège*, and you are even then miles away from the original. But if you are talking of a village school you must use the French word *école*. The French word *promenade* is used of a walk and also of any faring. It is used of an army marching during hostilities, but without the need of fighting. It is used of sailing out to sea in a boat. It is used of taking a horse out for exercise. But observe the grotesqueness of translating the French phrase in the latter case by the words *taking the horse out for a walk*. Literally, a Frenchman says, if you transliterate by the supposed equivalent, 'I was not on a voyage. I was only taking a walk out to sea.' You cannot translate that except by some such roundabout phrase as, 'I only went outside in my boat to-day.'

All this is negative, and leads to nothing by way of a conclusion, but there does arise from a consideration of all these difficulties a sort of working policy to be applied to translation; and it would seem to be this: first, to read your original until you have thoroughly got inside it, until you are part of it, as it were, or at least clothed with it, then to render into your own tongue freely and naturally the effect upon your mind, and then, in a third process, to compare the result with the original and bring them as close as may be, without leaving anything unnatural in the idiom of your translation, nor anything too shockingly untrue to the original.

But it is all very well to suggest this as a policy. The carrying out of it in practice is another matter. To do it perfectly a man would have to remember all that he had read and to keep a whole book like one picture before his eye, and that no man can do.

XX

On Witchcraft

I WAS RECENTLY READING A LEARNED MODERN
BOOK ON WITCHCRAFT. IT RAISED IN ME, AS I
read, a comment which may seem a little novel; although, paradoxically enough, the basis of that comment is a gross commonplace. Here is a careful,
scholarly, exact and thorough tabulation of evidence
upon the whole story of witchcraft in Western Europe, and especially in France and England, and I
confess that the greater the accumulation of evidence,
the greater the exactitude of the scholarship, the
more that comment recurs to my mind. It is the
comment that of all the marvels of the human story
the greatest is the total and rapid changes to which
the human mind is subject.

There are three common ways of approaching
the unnumbered evidences of magic in general, of
black magic in particular, and of witchcraft in Christendom especially.

The first is to believe in what one reads: to believe

such phenomena to be *real;* not the hallucinations of individuals, but true experiences thrust upon them by evil spirits. In a few this attitude comes of a reaction against the tiresome popular scepticism of our time; the attitude of the man who really believes, or persuades himself into half-believing, pretty well anything extraordinary when he knows the mass of his contemporaries reject it, especially if it seems to him picturesque. Intellectually this attitude is negligible, and the small number of people who go in for it generally grow out of it before they are thirty.

But there is another way of treating magic and witchcraft as real, and this way is very far from being negligible intellectually; indeed, is spreading rapidly, though here, also, it must be admitted that there is an element of reaction against the exasperating half-cultured negations of inferiors. It is the position taken by those who say that we must accept any great body of human testimony. It is applied not only to the old stories of witchcraft, but to the modern stories of spirits and apparitions; the modern necromancy of the spiritualists. The reasoning is on these lines: 'Of course, anything may be explained as an illusion. If a number of my fellow-beings testify that some strange phenomenon has given them a full sense of reality, I must accept their testimony just as I would accept it upon any other matter, although the particular thing to which they testify be unusual and by me unexperienced. I have no right to say that the whole mass of such convinced evidence is mere fancy.'

So much for the first way of approaching these affairs. The next way is the exact opposite. It is that of men who dogmatically deny the value of the evidence. No matter how numerous the examples or how solemn the declaration; no matter how much corroboration there may be of many confirming testimonies, it is all nonsense. If a thousand people see a thing, that is collective hallucination. If two people give corroborative evidence they are conspirators or liars, and if only one, then it is obviously an illusion. That is still the attitude of the great majority; but it is a dwindling majority.

The third method of regarding these things is much more difficult to maintain, and is held by very few. I am not quite sure that it is sincerely held by anybody, but at any rate it *professes* to be. A mere statement without conclusion, a mere interest in the fact that such things have been said and done, without pretence to decide whether they are true or false; whether, as the modern jargon goes, they were 'objective' or 'subjective.'

This purely negative attitude nearly always lapses into a quasi-scientific thesis closely allied to the second attitude. After accumulating great masses of evidence the accumulator goes on to connect the whole affair with some imaginary habits of primitive man and with the hypotheses (disguised as proved facts) wherewith all our generation has been stuffed: 'The survival of primitive ritual'—and all the rest of it.

Now all these attitudes are to me, I regret to say, indifferent; because each fails to apply the rule which reason should apply to all evidence of marvel, 'the greater the unlikelihood, the more need of evidence, and the stronger the quality and corroboration of it required.'

The second attitude, that of mere dogmatic denial, seems to me simply silly. A plumb dogma, affirmed without authority, is intellectually despicable; and that is the position of this dogma that things outside our own common experience cannot really exist. It is still very popular with the newly-enlightened masses, and that is all the more reason for despising it. A creed for which you cannot give your authority is a contradiction in terms: and there is here no authority, unless it be the supposed authority of print.

The third attitude is almost equally contemptible. Mere accumulation of evidence without decision is unworthy of the intelligence; and if the student inclines to substitute hypothesis for fact, why that is the intellectual disease of our time to be avoided like a physical plague. For it gives entry to the most degrading philosophies, and their most evil consequences upon society.

What these stories move in me is something very different. They move in me a quiet but unceasing wonder that the mind of man can so turn back upon and deny its own self. It does so not only in the matter of evil and its revelations (of possession, of black magic, of witchcraft, and the rest), it does so in much smaller things: in the effect of landscape, for instance, in the conception of beauty. I am not vastly impressed when I find the whole of a society (as in the seventeenth century) taking for granted whole batches of the marvellous. Nor am I greatly impressed when I find the whole of a society (as in the nineteenth century) vulgarly denying the marvellous. What does impress me is that this known instrument, the mind of man, which each of us possesses, which we each of us can closely examine, which seems in each of us to be so clear, so simply working within its boundaries, so absolute in its conclusions, can pass through such complete transformations.

The real difficulty of writing history lies in trying to call up within one's self (and having so called it up, to convey to one's reader) some past mood in our fathers of which he knows nothing, and of which we knew nothing until we took up our historical reading. The worst fault in history, infinitely worse than mechanical inaccuracy, and worse even than lack of proportion, is the fault of not knowing what the spiritual state of those whom one describes really was. Gibbon and his master Voltaire, the very best of reading, are for that reason bad writers of history. To pass through the tremendous history of the Trinitarian dispute from which our civilisation arose and to treat it as a farce is not history. To write the story of the sixteenth century in England and to make of either the Protestant or the Catholic a grotesque is to miss history altogether.

For some reason we cannot understand, one whole view of the world, one whole system of emotions will be taken for granted; then, a few generations later, that view, those emotions, will have become as alien as the things of another planet.

One would think it impossible to stand on the Mont d'Or above Vallorbe, looking towards the great mountains beyond the Lake of Geneva, and feel no religious awe. Yet we know how men no further than the grandfathers of our grandfathers looked on such a sight. They thought of it as we think of a tempestuous night on foot in the mud. The mountains were boring and intolerable obstacles to travel —and for nearly all men then they were nothing else. The use of torture in a court of law is incomprehensible to us. Those who relied upon it would find the immunity of wealthy men to-day equally amazing.

A man has but to live his half-century to see the process of change at work. It is like watching a clock, the hand of which moves too slowly to be perceived, but which, if one waits awhile, one discovers to have moved. There are books published to-day and familiarly read in England which, only thirty years ago, would have ensured the imprisonment of author and printer. There are things done to-day in public life which would have seemed merely fantastic to the men of Gladstone's generation. On the other hand, Pitt, sick with drink behind the Speaker's chair, a child hanged for theft as a matter of course a hundred years ago, are equally fantastic in our eyes.

To tell the honest truth, my private interest in the affair of magic, of possession, of witchcraft, and the rest, my historical interest—and I hope I shall not be thought too cynical—is a speculation upon whether I shall live to see the return of such belief. Men now alive, the younger men, will almost certainly see it. You have only to note what any particular time takes for granted as obvious and beyond discussion, to be certain that a nearly succeeding time will be as confident of the opposite.

XXI

The Man Who Lashed Out

HIS LORDSHIP THE MAYOR OF BILGETON HAD
BROKEN WITH HIS RULE NOT TO APPEAR IN
party politics during his year of office. He had con-
sented to preside over the vast meeting gathered in
the Jubilee Hall to welcome Mr. Michael Firley;
for the occasion was a very grave one, a farewell
honour to the great public man who was their Member of Parliament, and who was now retiring after an
honourable and unbroken service of twenty-two years
in the Commons.

His Lordship the Lord Mayor of Bilgeton introduced the speaker of the evening in a few well-
chosen words, which I will summarize in *oratio
obliqua*.

They were gathered there to-night, not as Liberals
or Conservatives, still less as supporters of the Labour Party (*laughter*), but as Englishmen, to welcome one of the greatest Englishmen of our time,
and one who had honoured—he thought he might

172

say honoured—the city of Bilgeton by accepting its freedom upon a recent occasion (*applause*). He did not believe in long speeches from the Chairman upon such an occasion as this (*Cries of 'Go on!'*), but he would be lacking in respect to the etc., etc., etc., if he did not, etc., etc., etc. The career of Mr. Firley— if he were still plain Mr. Firley he was sure that was through his own choice (*cheers*)—was a household word throughout the Empire and wherever the English language, etc., etc., etc. He could not forbear, etc., etc., etc., from, etc., etc., etc., and, etc., etc., etc., such as has made us what we are (*loud cheers*).

His Lordship then called upon Mr. Firley, a tall, lanky man, scholarly, a gentleman, only grey, yet over sixty; spare—already weary of this world; but in whose eyes might be perceived this evening a strange gleam.

Upon the rising of their Member the vast audience heaved to its myriad feet and sang, 'For he's a Jolly Good Fellow' to the tune of 'Malbrook,' and in all the keys adapted to the great variety of voices present. They concluded with three loud cheers, under each of which Mr. Firley raised one eyebrow and depressed the other in a quick, nervous movement, of which he was not the master.

When stuffy silence had fallen, the man whose

career was ending coughed slightly, balanced his eye-glass on his left forefinger, and delivered himself of the following words:

'Men of Bilgeton, When I see you here before me in such numbers, and consider to what ages you have succeeded, what a story there lies behind that generation of which you are the ephemeral members, of what centuries you are the latest crown (*cheers*), I am moved to regard you, not without a certain awe, not without a certain pity, but also with a picture in my mind of very different things, very different places, very different men. Those of whom you are the sons and (little as you know it) the heirs, crowd before me. I recall what heritage of beauty lay to your hands as to those of all our race, what wealth of wisdom, what established laughter, what consolation in tears. It was for you the Charioteer came out of Asia driving the panther team, and for you that the Paphian broke into her youngest smiles. It was for you, and to bring you forth, the latest fruit of time, that the gods on their cloudy summits to the North conceived the mighty parents of the world. O, harvest of what unnumbered æons! O, heirs of what an inheritance! (*Loud cheers.*)

'I know not how it is, but in the contemplation of your economy (when my mind dwells on it from within), in the contemplation of your dwellings, of what were once, I suppose (and perhaps still are), your places of worship, of the ornaments you are pleased to use for the variety of your dress, when my corporeal eyes dwell upon these externals of your lives, I muse! I find something inexplicable. Am I in a bewilderment for things, lost? Am I gazing across too wide a gulf of years? Or do I dwell in a world that is other than the world we seem to see? I know not. . . . But I am in an admiration of what time can effect (*applause*).

'It was but some few days ago that I filled a leisured evening—the day had been fine, the air in the declining light was still, the prospect clear—that I filled an evening, I say, with gazing from the heights of the moor above down into your busy valley. I saw rising from lowering belts of coal smoke (*cheers*) the tall chimneys of Messrs. Hailey-bury's Limited (*loud and prolonged cheers*), the considerable expanse of the railway station roof, sub-fusc—nay, "grisatre." I caught a glimpse of the narrow river confined between brick walls of now respectable antiquity (*cheers*), but the distance was too great to allow me to perceive the details of what objects might be floating upon that historic stream. From the general hum of the great hive there came occasionally sharp sounds detached—the clang of an electric tram, and, at their appointed hour, the indiscriminate hooting of many sirens (*laughter and cheers*). I could also faintly catch the peculiar shrill cry of newsvendors, and at irregular but frequent intervals there pierced through, in vivid stabs, the warning whistles of locomotives.

'But all this I saw and heard as upon a background of other things: first, the valley itself contained no more than a few thatched homes of yeomen; the river turned one mill, and that for corn; there were sheep upon the higher pastures. Far away, in some fashion general, as it were, and sustaining it all, was a boundary of mighty and beneficent sea waters informed with the Mediterranean air. Great roads had impressed upon a wide landscape the spirit of a mighty soldiery, and Authority brooded over the whole. Authority it was, Authority which gave regularity to every shrine and every habitation, every domestic custom, every law: to the plains, to the mountains, to the souls of men. I saw all this first dimly guarded by beneficent powers not of this world, which later changed to have evil faces, but fled at last before the strong, dim forms of the Saints (*cheers*). I heard the clash of armies, but they were the armies of Christian men, and I saw

176

fantastic loveliness arise in garment and in brick and in wood and in stone.

'All these things I saw as a man may see a vision; I looked for its fruits—but the vision faded. There lay before me—Bilgeton (*loud and prolonged cheers*).

'I have nothing more to say. Nor would I have spoken as I have—I trust that I have not wearied you by any obscurity or by allusions that might be unfamiliar to you (*cries of 'No, no!'*)—had I not determined to put a term to the career of one whom you have fondly believed (*cheers*) to be your representative (*loud cheers*). Or rather, had not such an occasion been provided for me by others.

'My Lord Mayor (*turning to that official*) was good enough to remark that I was plain Mr. Firley. I can no longer conceal from you that the necessity of finding a seat of the safest kind for the nephew of Lady Cumbledown (*loud cheers*) has—by I know not what association of ideas—suggested to his Majesty the conferring upon me of a peerage under the style and title which has graciously been granted me of Bilgeton (*loud and prolonged cheers, during which the vast audience again heaved to its myriad feet and attempted in some confusion to renew the former chorus, while Mr. Firley wearily waved them*

177

down with his hand and at last obtained a hearing).
Nay, fellow-citizens, if I may so call you (*cheers*).
Men, Bilgetonians, do not be too eager to congratulate me on what will be but the last phase of an
exhausted life. (*No! No!*) For I make no pretence to that concealment of age which is the vulgar
fashion of our day. I go to a peerage, due to I know
not what, but you to the daily life of Bilgeton, and,
as Socrates has said through the mouth of Plato (or
Plato through the mouth of Socrates), who can tell
which fate is the better? In the greater leisure that
is now before me (I have not hesitated to accumulate
out of politics what I thought necessary for the se-
curity of my later years) I shall return to communion with the Classics, to the occasional enjoyment
of a picture or a statue, to the rarer consolation of
reasonable converse—perhaps, who knows (it would
be good fortune indeed)—with a true human friend.
What will follow after I know not, neither do any
of you; for the things beyond this world the gods
have hidden from human eyes.' (*Tempest of
cheers.*)

The right honourable gentleman abruptly sat
down, after having spoken for seventeen minutes
and thirty-five seconds.

His Lordship the Mayor said, when the thunder

of cheering had gradually died down (I again use the *oratio obliqua*), that they had all enjoyed an intellectual treat. They could not all be scholars like Mr. Firley (*cheers*); they could not all—least of all he himself (*cries of 'No, no!'*)—claim to express themselves with the same facility, etc., etc., etc., when their children and their children's children's children, etc., etc., etc., of this great Empire (*more and still louder cheers, at the conclusion of which the vast audience heaved for a third time to its feet and for the third time intoned their familiar choral salutation, to which Mr. Firley listened with a look of patient agony, and acknowledged with a slight apathetic bow from his stooping figure*).

XXII

On Lucidity

MAN WHEN HE SETS TO WORK HAS AN OBJECT IN HIS WORK. WHEN HE BUILDS HIS OBJECT is to protect beings and goods from the weather. When he imitates the human form or landscape in the plastic arts his object is to record an impression and to fix the passage of life; to defeat time. When he writes his object is to express a conception; that is, to give it such exact substance as shall permit him to convey it to others.

But even as he works man finds that his activity becomes, *must be*, a *construction*. He cannot work at large. He must work in a manner. And this is true because he is limited and because what is creative in him is a personality. Whatever he makes in building or in delineation or in written expression approaches perfection through the recognition of those two things, limitation and the unity inseparable from an individual soul creating. If in his eagerness he neglects limit, his effect is spoilt. If from whatever influence of fatigue or of confusion he loses unity, his effect is spoilt. Whatever he makes, therefore, tends to be, in proportion to his success, a united thing, with an outline and a character of its own reflecting or projecting the limited, strictly homogeneous thing from which it came: a human soul.

Man, recognizing this, fully aware (especially in the old age of art) that what he makes must bear a constructional character, begins to run a risk of the error opposite to neglect or confusion. He begins to give form the first place and to make his effort an attempt at form rather than an attempt at expression and creation. He is tempted to substitute the secondary for the primary thing.

In the history of letters, now the one error, now the other, has prevailed. In the time in which we live and in the medium which we use to-day for expression, the English language, the error has run to the very extreme of neglect and confusion. Side by side with this there runs, indeed, by way of protest, a little perpetual accompaniment of the companion error, the exaggeration of form. But looseness is the rule; and it seems to me that the first criticism to be made of modern working English is that it has lost the sense of form; but the very next criticism immediately to be added is that our attempt to re-establish form should be vividly upon its guard against preciosity. A generation ago we had the two things very distinct. We had the influx (which has since broadened) of a chaotic flood of English, appearing especially in fiction. And as fiction became the more and more exaggerated type of general reading the looseness grew with it. Men and women grew famous for their fiction because it suited so the passing mood, though it was shapeless. The incentive to a permanent manner was thus weakened and the formlessness began to cover the field. Side by side with this there was the little school of which Henley was a leader and Stevenson the most famous craftsman, who in their reaction against splosh tended to arrange words in patterns. Both were wrong, but the first were much the more wrong of the two and continued to be more wrong.

To get to the marrow of the thing we have first to ask ourselves why a man writes prose—for I am speaking of prose, not verse; the problem of form in verse is quite a different one. You may say that he writes prose to maintain his miserable existence, which is true enough; and very little prose would be written if wealth were better distributed. But when I ask 'why,' I mean with what 'prose-writing object' is prose written? It is written to convey the conception of the writer—a conclusion, an idea, or a vision —to the mind of the reader.

What, then, is its principal quality, by which it always should be tested? *Lucidity* in the full sense of the word; and lucidity does not mean ease of appreciation by the stupidest reader or by the reader with the smallest vocabulary; nor does it mean the expression of ideas which are more easily grasped than others. It means that quality in prose whereby whatever you have had in your mind, however difficult to convey, however unusual, however much requiring the use of terms which may be unfamiliar, shall in the highest degree of clarity possible reappear in your reader's mind. Not all things can be conveyed with an equal degree of lucidity, but the highest degree of lucidity proper to each is the goal. I cannot convey the idea of a hyperbola as clearly to all minds as I can convey the idea of a circle, but there is such a theory as an exact, clear and simple definition of the hyperbola.

A German of a hundred years ago said very truly that the art of writing was to get the words down on the paper so that they could rise again from the paper alive into the reader's soul. To do that is to be lucid, and everything in a man's prose which makes that prose less lucid than it need be is a defect.

If it comes from clumsiness or inability, it is an involuntary defect and may, upon analysis, be corrected. If it is voluntarily assumed, it is a sin against the canons of good writing.

Many do so assume it as a short cut to reputation. They are the worst enemies of a national literature. Since novel thought falls easily into novel expression, and since deep thought is arrived at in the mind of the writer through a struggle, the one and the other (and especially both combined) tend to be obscurely expressed. The obscurity can be more and more eliminated by a greater and greater mental effort, by that 'fundamental brain work' which Rossetti postulated as the first test of writing worth reading. Often it cannot be wholly eliminated, from the very nature of the subject dealt with; but it can be eliminated in a greater and greater degree the more trouble a man takes, and the more he fixes himself upon the reader and the less he entangles himself in his own vanity. That is why it has been said with great truth that a man having something to say, intensely desiring to say it, and burning with the passion to make others accept it, cannot write ill; or, at any rate, in proportion to his powers, his chances of writing ill are definitely less than those of a man with little to say and indifferent to its acceptance.

But because great things have so often, in their author's haste, been said obscurely, and yet have still been recognized for great things, therefore imitators bring in the detestable habit of affected and voluntary obscurity. Browning's writing, especially his later writing (which certainly was prose and not verse), is an example in point; and Carlyle would like to have been obscure in imitation of the dull gods he worshipped; but there was such an energy in the man that he clarified his impression in spite of himself and baked the German mud with Scottish fire.

There are in this supreme character of lucidity two kinds, and the great writers always combine both. There is the general lucidity, which informs whole pages and a work throughout its course. There is the particular and sacred lucidity of lapidary phrase: the junction of some few words which flood the mind with light, raising up a whole age upon their small foundation. Here you have a parallel to what happens with good draftsmanship in the hands of genius. I will be so old-fashioned as to cite a parallel from the art of Raphael, whom fools called Sanzio. If you will look at the Sistine Madonna (which I am afraid is still in Dresden) you will see that there is accurate line throughout. What that man intended to convey by line he conveyed.

He was the master and creator of his line. He did not allow it to react upon and influence him. The majesty of the Woman's face, the charm of the two little faces at the foot, are creations exactly according to the intent of their creator, as is the movement of the drapery and the composition as a whole. But there is in this combination of lucidities a singular, exceptional, ecstatic success: I mean the eyes of the Child. In the delineation of these the draftsmanship transcends itself and suggests things beyond the world: such transcendence is the occasional triumph of lucidity.

Now in prose you have the same. The business of the prose writer is to convey. His instrument must be completely his servant and must never, in however little, control its master. He must not say a thing to suit that instrument. He must compel the instrument to suit his needs. But even as he does so, and because lucidity has been his honest and continued intention, there will be granted to him over and over again, in points like jewels, the lapidary phrase.

Thus Newman, who without a doubt possessed beyond any other writer in English of our time this prime quality of prose writing, runs like a broad and full river, page upon page, and yet inevitably strikes one gleam after another which a lesser man would have attempted deliberately to form as though he were writing not prose, but rhetoric or verse. In what I conceive to be the best example of general prose we possess—I mean the four canonical Gospels —it is astonishing with what frequency these summits rise from the general level. It is remarkable that the four canonical Gospels, if they be carefully translated into any tongue, seem to retain their supreme quality; something which is not true of any other work I know—certainly not of the rest of Scripture. I have been told, indeed, that the Epistles of St. Paul can be rendered by a good Hellenist into something like English prose, but I have not seen the experiment succeed. The Gospels are a monument of prose. And in them you get those lapidary phrases which are the crown of lucidity over and over again: 'Fear not, I have overcome the world,' or again, 'They knew Him in the breaking of bread.' If a man be asked, then, for a simple rule whereby prose would be constructively written, should be a thing made, and therefore enduring, I think the best answer would be what I have suggested. Consider only the reaching of your reader and *develop* that.

For every quality of good prose proceeds from that. You cannot reach your reader properly unless you have ordered your own ideas. You cannot in decency affect to reach him unless you have something worthy of his acceptance. In other words, this rule guarantees that you will have something to say and that this something will be a thing and not a mist. All the little tricks whereby we improve the use of a language: the suppression of tautology; the difficult placing of the relative; the choosing of the exact word which by all its connotations reveals the idea in our mind; the balance of the sentence, not too long to fatigue attention, yet not barbarically short as though one were addressing a fool or a child; the making of the sentence of just that rhythm which shall express the proportion between the main idea and its modification; even the balance of the paragraph and of the whole work—all fall under this rule.

There falls under it the excision of redundancy, which is the curse of an otiose style. To be redundant comes from being slothful or too hurried; and it is bad to be redundant in prose, because redundancy confuses the mind of the reader, *not* because it makes the writer ridiculous, though it does that, too. I may be asked how this general rule touches what is certainly a supreme quality in all prose—to wit, a right sense of intonation and inflexion. I answer that this will come of itself from the desire to express. For expression is of itself a musical thing. But if you seek it as an object in itself, then your prose will be saccharine, which is a dreadful thing for prose to be. Herein also Walter Pater erred and Bergson is a great sinner.

Some imagine that this rule of lucidity attaches only to statement; that is, to prediction. It has a much wider, a universal application. It attaches to irony, to indignation, to the pathetic, to the enthusiastic, to the subdued. It attaches to every mood properly belonging to your expression, for your expression is only achieved if that mood is aroused in the mind of the reader as in your own.

But the moment a man turns the process right about face and seeks a verbal effect for its own sake, calculating a rhythm or introducing a word for the purpose of exhibition, his prose corrupts. This does not mean that many a writer who clearly wrote good prose has not an odd effect, but it does mean that he had an odd effect in spite of himself. Meredith is most powerful because he is continually determined to express and get his reader to receive what he desires to give. He is as clearly working in a material which strains him. One good critic said that 'he thought in a foreign language,' but he had no *intention* of the grotesque. The intention of Meredith is sincere, and the sincerity of his intention is what gives him his place.

There is a test for prose, as for all human works, which is the test of time. Prose which a man has determined to make lucid is necessarily constructed prose. It is something made. It cannot but work within limits and develop of itself its outline. It has an edge and is hard and endures. And the worst penalty we can attach to the unconstructed writing of our day is to tell its authors that quite certainly they will not survive. A popularity among millions, a facile agreement with readers whom the author pretends to lead, but whom in reality he anxiously follows, an erroneous judgment that little interests of your moment are permanent human interests— all these come under the test of time. There is no mass of formless writing in the past by which we can judge the truth of this. Formless writing is a modern thing. But we can test the truth of it by the converse error of precious writing. What has survived from the seventeenth and eighteenth centuries has been matter possessing form through the desire to convey. The finicky work has perished. The carefully arranged maze of words has become intolerably tedious. It had a vast success in its own time; posterity found it hopeless. And so it will be, I am certain, with our opposite extreme to-day. Posterity will find our formlessness intolerable, and the stuff marred by it will die, however famous now. It will give the impression not of voices speaking, but of mere noise. But where, here and there in our babel, a clear and individual voice speaks with proper modulation, with a natural but conspicuous rhythm, with a vocabulary consonant to the matter to be expressed, without tricks, without lassitude, and disdaining to sprawl, that voice will survive. Such oases alone will stand out of the Sahara of modern rubbish. But they are few and they are getting fewer.

XXIII

The Bastard's Book

I HAVE ALWAYS LOVED WILLIAM THE BASTARD OF FALAISE. HE DIED SO LONG AGO THAT MY affection for him is of no material use to me, and his family came to an end, in the male line, with that drunken shipwreck off Calvados—which shows the importance of large families and the folly of getting drunk before you are in deep water. I have loved him for his grand manner, for his bullet head and short hair (by which he never let himself be caught), for his violent affair with his cousin in his youth, and his fidelity in manhood; for going to pieces when she died after a long lifetime; for his gigantic temper, and for his admirable death. I hope I shall have a deathbed as good as that.

He was to blame, I know, in many things. He was much too cruel to North Yorkshire and Durhame, though it is true they had exasperated him. And he was too particular about money. Also he only swore one oath, which seems to me to mark a lack of vocabulary. Further, he made the mistake of trusting people who liked him, instead of trusting the people whom he liked; and that is why he saddled this island with the brave but disreputable and vicious son who did no good.

So I say I have ever loved William. Nevertheless, there was a day some years ago when I was inclined to take him amiss and lose something of my respect for the shadow of that great name.

The thing arose in this manner. There was, in connection with William of Falaise, a certain point which I had to decide to my own satisfaction, and, having read many books upon this point, I came upon one book at last which really did tell me something, and on which a sentence or two of history might be written without falsehood—and that is rare. So I set out in the morning to go into London from Kensington with this book—I will not say under my arm (for it was too big for that), but I carried it as one would carry a framed picture. I climbed with it onto the tops of 'buses, I plunged with it into the depths of the Tube. I said to myself: 'This is the day on which the great passage must be written and the doubtful point concluded for ever. This mighty tome which I bear shall be consulted in my first moment of leisure, and all Europe will rejoice.'

Note you, I was not going to copy what this book said. I was going to find out from this book what the truth was, although the book did not agree with it. I was going to discover from this book, in the teeth of its author, and in spite of him, what really happened in the matter which had perplexed me. Therefore did I stagger under its weight through so many miles, far above and far below the common pavement of imperilled London. Reaching that place where I thought I could find repose, I spread the volume out upon a desk, and taking a fair white sheet of paper and a pen, I was ready for the great conclusion. But at that moment there came in a small child with a message from the telephone bidding me attend like a slave in the presence of a superior—or, at any rate, of a man very much wealthier than I. I was tempted to leave the great book on the desk and come back to it after the considerable journey I was thus bound to take, far within the bounds of the city; but I said to myself: 'No, I shall find a moment of freedom, I shall be able to go into a coffee-house during business hours when there will be nobody there. My pen is a fountain pen (for I am abreast of the times); I will also take with me my fair sheet of paper, and there will I conclude my business. Moreover, on my journey I will be able to read the Great Book and store my mind, and, best of all, when I have done with it in the City, I will be able to make a parcel of it and send it on to my home, and be rid of its abominable weight.' Therefore did I go off with the monument of William the Bastard of Falaise, again held awkwardly, and once more from the heights of 'buses and from the depths of Tubes it accompanied me like the millstone round the neck of the scandal-giver.

As I entered the Presence, my superior facetiously remarked that I seemed to be carrying a big book, and asked me what it was about. I told him it was about William the Conqueror, and avoided any fine phrases about Falaise, bastardy, fidelity, courage, temper, a good death, and the rest. When he heard it was about William the Conqueror an expression of no-enthusiasm entered his eyes, and he went to the matter in hand. He took hours over it: it was about the sailing of a ship, and what had to be done with regard to that sailing. Had *I* been *his* superior I could have got it over in five minutes, but these wealthy men take their time. Indeed, they never seem to me to do any work, and that, I suppose, is why they are so rich. For it has been properly debated, but never concluded, whether men are most impoverished by industry or good judgment, or most enriched by laziness or by folly.

At last he let me go, and with another joke upon my book, more ponderous than the book itself, dismissed me.

It was late, but not yet the luncheon hour; so I said to myself that I should get a table free. I went into the coffee-house; I humbly took a table at the very back of the place where it was dark, but with electric light above me. I ordered some chemical coffee which they serve in such places. I put out my paper, I lifted my pen. Then the young woman who presided over this end of the room switched off the light. I patiently waited her return; she brought me the coffee. I begged her to switch on the light again; she did so under some protest; but hardly had she done so when people began to pour in. It was the moment when the wretched dependents of the rich gamblers come in to eat too little too hurriedly. One of these, a large fine fellow, handsome, too, and full of initiative, sat down at my own table; and though he did not say anything, very properly looked reprovingly at my book, which covered it. So I shut it up again, put it on the floor beside me, drank my coffee and went out.

By this time I was about as angry with William of Falaise as the Aetheling might be, but not more. It was but a small simmering anger, and I made allowances as justice demanded, recognizing that he was not to blame. I said to myself: 'I will take this book back to my hotel, there I will lunch, and after lunch I will go into a small smoking-room which I know of, and there will I spread out my big book and decide the mighty controversy which has torn historians for more than a hundred years.'

So I staggered out again under my big burden, and had the great difficulty in finding the coins to pay with and in holding the volume at the same time, and once more did I go—but this time westward—above and below the too narrow and congested streets of London, until at last I entered the place I spoke of, and there I spread out the big book and the fair paper, and invoked whatever Muse it is that looks after the beastly and impecunious business of history, and was ready. But three men—Canadians—came in and sat immediately beside me and talked in the most cheerful manner on shipping. They were either men who were going to make money by shipping, or they were men who were impressing each other about shipping. At any rate, shipping was not anything I wanted to hear about just then, and the association was unpleasant to my mind after what I had just gone through.

I tried to follow what was in the big book, but, instead of that, with the very first words of the sentence I found my mind hooked on to the interesting point of whether the *Ooronoka* would or would not fit into the canal. A younger or more courageous man would here have said: 'I hope to God she sticks fast in the lock and stays there, and then perhaps we shall have a little peace!' But an older and less courageous man did nothing of the sort. He wearily took up the gigantic burden and, finding it quite intolerable, was at the expense of a taxi, saying to himself: 'I will go to a friend's house, and there will I nail down William of Falaise for ever.'

Before I got to the friend's house it began to rain. I paid off the taxi—I had no umbrella—the rain fell upon me abominably, but also, I am glad to say, upon William of Falaise.

That great soldier never minded the weather, in which character he resembled all great soldiers I ever heard of; he went through the Pennines in the snow of March, with all the *brio* of Napoleon crossing the Guadarrama, and under the same threat of mutiny. Remembering this, I knew that the rain would do him no harm, but I was savage enough by this time to hope it would wet him. It was astonishing how long they kept William and me outside that door. At last it opened: I asked whether I might not in that house, where I was so familiar, be allowed to work in a room which I knew to be empty. I was going to say that I desired to disturb no one, when the great personage who opened the door to me, looking at me with a mixture of solemnity and disfavour, asked me if I had not heard.

What I had not heard was that the house was a prey to violent contagious disease, and that one of its dearest occupants was already in danger of his life. I left anxious messages and tramped through the rain to the nearest cab-stand, considering as I did so how expensive the victor of Val-es-Dunes was becoming. I consoled myself with the thought that the cab-stand was quite close. When I got there, there were no cabs; they had all been taken by the rich. I walked on further, quite a long way, and at last I found a cab crawling. I got into it, forgot that I had not told the man where I wanted to go. At random I mentioned another hotel where I happened to know that there was usually a quiet public room. It was a long way off, and it would cost a great deal to get there. At any rate, I should at last be able to tackle the principal business of my life.

The cab started; it was an extraordinarily bad cab; the tyres were bad, the springs were pretty well gone, and the engines did not work properly. Halfway through that road which divides Hyde Park from Kensington Gardens the cab stopped with a grinding noise, and the driver got off to see what was the matter with its inside. I sat there a full five minutes, with only William for company, and he dead. Then I thought I would get out, pay off the man and get another cab. I got out, paid off the man, but I did not get another cab, because the rain, which was now coming down like Noah's, had caused everyone in London who could afford a cab to pick one up. There went past me many cabs, but not one with its flag up.

By this time I hated William of Falaise as bitterly as ever he was hated by old Freeman, let alone by Stigand in his later years, though I must say he treated Stigand well—too well. I should have got rid of the fellow altogether, and I am not sure I should not have cut off his head; but that is by the way. All the way across the bridge, and down to Exhibition Road, did I stagger with the book, saying to myself: 'I will get an omnibus and find some place of repose.'

It was at this moment that to my infinite joy a friend passed in a motor car, so opulent, so large, so secure against the weather, that it seemed like the Garden of the Lord to the rebel horde in the American rhyme. I waved at the rich man; he took me in; he said: 'I do not know where you want to go, but I am in a hurry, I have to go to Victoria, and when I have taken my train, I will send the car wherever you want.' I thanked him very courteously and thought him a godsend. When we got to Victoria, I knew it was only decent to get out and see my friend to the train. In other words, I did a good deed; and as everybody knows, or ought to know, a good deed produces heavy consequences. I saw my friend into the train all right; there he was in a Pullman, with a fine great cigar and the happy face of those who are blessed by the Devil in this world. I left him and hurried back to his car.

It was gone, and William with it!

Then I went to a neighbouring shrine of my acquaintance, and registered a curse thus:

'O William of Falaise, I will have nothing to do with you any more! O faithful husband! O too

indulgent father! O devout dier! O mighty soldier! O energetic exclaimer of the single oath and
swearer by the Splendour of God! I will wish you
nothing worse than that you and I shall never hear
of each other again! I did not follow you to the
house of the rich man, for I am absolutely certain
by the time I get there through the pouring rain,
or at the expense of yet another taxi, it will turn
out that the car is not there, but has gone to the
garage, for the rich man being away for the week-
end, the chauffeur will certainly be making an honest
penny by hiring it out to others. I will not bother
to discover you again, enormous book; I am well
rid of you. I am indifferent to your hero, and I
will put him out of my mind for ever, and ever,
and for ever.

'And this book which records him I devote to the
gods below.'

I went off. But when I got home, to my sad and
distant room at evening, there was William of
Falaise, soaked with rain, splashed with mud; and
on the top of that, the very next Monday, I came
across the chauffeur who had returned it, and I had
to give him half a crown.

XXIV

On Macaulay

THE OTHER DAY I HAD OCCASION TO RE-READ MACAULAY'S "HISTORY" IN THE MATTER OF James II. I had to do this, not because Macaulay had anything new to tell me—he never had anything new to tell anybody—but because I wanted to see how the conventional enemy looked at the affair.

It was more than twenty-five years since I had read him, and how fresh he came! It is to the glory of this facile rhetorician that after half an active lifetime since a last reading, and more than a lifetime from his first writing, it is all still as clear and clean and fresh as reasonably good water out of a large tap in the public washhouse of a well-appointed industrial town. I would not, indeed, compare it to a mountain spring; but it is quite as clean and clear and fresh as the water you get out of such a tap in the above-mentioned well-appointed industrial town.

There are two very good rules, I think, to apply when the question is asked whether a man is a good writer: the first is whether he carries you on and makes you continue the reading of him; the second is whether he remains alive after a long space of time—and on this second point there are two criteria: first, how much he remains alive to you after many years of your own age since first you read him; and, secondly, how much he remains alive after a long space of time since first he wrote: after more than a generation.

Now, under both these tests, Macaulay comes out very well indeed. It is as fresh and vigorous reading to me in the decline of life as it was to me in youth, and it is as fresh and vigorous reading to the man of to-day in the London of petrol and an immense income-tax and cads in control as it was in the London of the great Whig houses and the carriages and pairs, and a government of gentlemen. Is not that a remarkable thing to say of any man? Is it not a feather in the cap of any man who wrote so long ago, who lived in so narrow a world, and who addressed himself to a public all of whom *and all of whose certitudes* are now dead?

It is remarkable not only as an evidence of vitality in writing, but as a mere linguistic feat. All the middle and early Victorians are already dating—

except Macaulay (and the earlier poems of Tenny-son). Some of the middle Victorians do not date, and perhaps never will; Huxley, for instance. But the earlier people do—except Macaulay. I suppose upon examination it will be found that this con-servation of him is due—largely, at least—to his use of words as natural to him as to the ordinary English reader. What else it may be due to I know not. But there it is. His philosophy is as dead as mutton; his doctrines are a jest; the falsehoods in which he delighted—representation, competition, impeccable judges, *habeas corpus*—(they are still repeated in our textbooks, but it is now ritual alone) are found out and quite discredited; what was *his* delight in large brick towns of the north and the midlands has be-come *our* nausea; his conception of government by the rich as a sort of paradise is not accepted even by the rich themselves to-day. Yet he does not date.

Macaulay's great quality is ease. He is like a man who sits down to dinner with friends all of whom are thoroughly his own; nothing he can say will offend them; they agree beforehand with the statements they are about to hear from him. The domestics in the house, the mahogany furniture, the beastly curtains, the uneatable food, are all to him as delightful as they are familiar. He is not like a man speaking in his own home; he is like a man visiting and eating with friends in a circle of some dozen houses, each of which will mirror exactly his own self-satisfied vanity, and as exactly his own raw and absurdly insufficient convictions. For Macaulay, like all his kindred, reposed upon a whole haystack of dogmas, not one of which he knew to be a dogma. He took them for granted as part of the universe. Where people differed from him he simply thought they could not see.

But in connexion with that last point, there arises a most important moral question. When Macaulay lied—and God knows he lied freely!—how much was he to blame? I read in a translation made by a Frenchman from the Arabic this phrase spoken by an innocent man condemned to torture and death, and launched at the judge who had condemned him: 'Hell will be your end: but there is One who knows.' It was explained in a footnote the meaning concealed therein was a sort of Mohammedan humility—if that term be not too paradoxical. As who should say, 'It seems to me that you, most wicked Judge, will be damned; but only God really understands the hearts of men.'

How much, then, was Macaulay to blame? The

whole picture is false, and in numberless particular points there are particular falsehoods. For instance, he knew just as well as I do, and just as well as all contemporary Europe did, the moral character of William III. Yet he pretends indignation at any such gossip passing from one foul lip to another. He was, we may be quite certain, acquainted with the judgment passed by contemporary Europe on all that affair, and of why it was so judged. On the Battle of the Boyne and the whole Irish Campaign he is absurd: misstating the numbers, misstating the manœuvres, misstating their objects, misstating the results; suppressing the overwhelming superiority of the invaders in numbers, training, and, above all, artillery. On the Siege of 'Derry, he is ludicrously and impudently at issue with reality.

Again, he conceals from his readers all the natural and even obvious doubts upon Barillon's letter to Louis XIV concerning James's claim to the arrears of payment due. He does not, as Lingard does, go carefully into the question of Barillon's own commission, and the vehement desire that diplomat was under to get the money paid, for the sake of his own pocket.

Again, he talks vaguely of James II's 'filling'

the Bench and the University and the Army and heaven knows what else with Papists, when, as a fact, the proportion of posts so filled was far inferior to the numerical proportion which might have been demanded. In this connexion also (and here alone) Macaulay abandons all attempt at perspective and represents James's co-religionists as less than a seventh of their real number. It is a point where even the average schoolboy history, Green's for instance, has not the face to follow him. It is as grossly unhistorical as it would be to-day to say that teetotallers were a small fraction of the English people.

Well, in such instances as these—and one might multiply them indefinitely—how far is Macaulay morally to blame? In a general sense he cannot be too much blamed, for the whole virtue of history is to tell the truth. A historian who does not tell the truth, and who knows he is not telling the truth, is more to be blamed by the human race at large than almost any other dealer in falsehood. He does not destroy a particular man's liberty or fortune, as does a false witness or an official judge, but he perverts the national memory.

Yet there is a particular sense in which one must find some excuse. Macaulay did clearly hold a sort of irrational religion, blindly believed, un-analysed, a certain theory of the State. It is the theory called Whig. In its essence, as I have said, it is the idea that the rich should govern, and that the most horrible of all political evils is a popular monarchy strong enough to control the powerful and protect the oppressed. It is the theory of the mid-nineteenth century tea-table in the large country house. God rest its soul—for it also is dead.

Macaulay held that doctrine in full, not only as a principle, but in all its detailed applications. He was absolutely certain that in defending it he was defending eternal justice and eternal right and eternal everything else. He believed its truth was confirmed as by Divine revelation in the sudden, the sensational increase of wealth and numbers, brick houses and hideous furniture—to the last triumphs of which he was born.

Now when a man is arguing as a lawyer to a brief, though he be arguing for a cause in which he believes, yet is he drawn as by ropes towards making everything support his client. He will suppress, distort, and misstate—but all for the right side—and that is Macaulay's excuse.

It is a subtle point in moral theology (which those

may discuss who are interested in that science) how the very certitude of a major truth may lead a man to a lot of lying. But, at any rate, Macaulay was, in that largest matter of his creed, transparently sincere; and as a writer he has triumphantly survived.

XXV

On the Word 'Scientific'

THERE NEVER WAS SUCH A TIME AS OUR OWN FOR THE USE OF MAGICAL WORDS DIVORCED from reason and used as talismans.

There is the word 'Democracy'; there is 'Progress'; there is 'All Authorities are agreed'; and there is 'Recent research has established'; but I think the worst of all is the word 'Scientific.' It is used with a force of finality and though, once used, all discussion ended. A thing having been said to be established 'Scientifically' there is no more questioning of it. An opponent having been proved unscientific is out of Court.

Now, it is noticeable that of this word, as of all the other exceedingly unintelligent talismans or magic formulæ in this our newspaper epoch, a definition is not attempted. The word is used like the name of a tribal god, to overawe an opponent; but those who use it neither think out what it means nor perhaps are capable of thinking it out. If they did, they would not advance what they call 'Scientific proof,' which does not prove at all, nor call that form of proof 'Unscientific,' which is in deed and truth the most scientific of any. For instance, they would not call a fall in the death-rate 'Scientific proof' of better health in the community. It is nothing of the sort. It is a proof of a longer average life, which longer average life may be increasingly unhealthy. They would not call the clear judgment of general observation in the matter 'Unscientific.' It is the best evidence in the world.

The word 'Science' means knowledge arrived at by some form of convincing proof, the better in quality the more convincing. For instance, we all know that there is a great mass of people travelling into London by the main terminal stations in the morning and travelling out of it in the evening; that knowledge is not 'Scientific.' We have all observed these crowds. To assert that they exist is scientific in the fullest sense of the word. It does not become more scientific in proportion as we examine all the evidence tabulated, all the suggestions we can get which coordinate the numbers coming in and going out with a time-table of hours, mark the various destinations, and so forth. When we have established a fairly large body of such information, properly sifted and put into its order, we may be said to have a more exhaustive and detailed knowledge of the human ebb and flow by rail into and out of London during the working day. But if in the course of juggling with figures you work it out that the volume of such traffic is not startlingly great, you are grossly unscientific. So far from advancing the area of knowledge you are proposing a falsehood and backing it upon sophistry. Thus, if you showed that of the total population only a small percentage so moved every morning and evening, it would still be true that the actual volume was most striking, that it particularly impresses one by its increase, and that its concentration adds to the effect.

A parallel example of the false 'Scientific' is the pretence that, because an instantaneous photograph of a horse at full gallop is quite different from a good artist's drawing of it, the artist is wrong. Quite the contrary. He is right. He is trusting to the best of all evidence, his own senses; and his co-ordination of a thousand movements is something the camera could never give, but is, indeed, what *is*. He gives you a horse *galloping:* not artificially halted in one-hundredth of a second, within which limits no human sense can work.

Again, when you have acquired organised knowledge of a numerical sort you have only touched a small part of the body of questions to which discussion attaches; but organised knowledge, that is, 'Science' and 'scientific method,' ought to be carried into all of them—and that is just where the modern use of the words 'Science' and 'Scientific' chiefly fails. It is applied to that kind of evidence which is strictly measurable and especially to that which is mechanical. It is not applied to any one of the other innumerable departments of evidence, nor is distinction made between the different kinds of things which have to be proved.

For instance, a man will give you 'scientific' proof —it is quite easy to do—that eating beefsteaks or drinking beer is a deadly habit. He will accumulate statistics of people who have eaten beefsteaks and drunk beer and who have died shortly after; of the cancer-curve in countries where they eat beefsteaks and drink beer compared with countries where they only eat vegetables and drink water; of the longer expectation of life in babies who don't than in adults who do, and so on. It is only too easy for the most unintelligent man to draw up any number of such tables, and they are all ridiculous and misleading because they omit the chief piece of evidence, which is that of our daily lives. We know by our own experience and that of people round us that, with us at least, in the English climate, the eating of butcher meat and drinking ale is a normal experience which goes well with a happy and a healthy life. But that kind of evidence cannot be exactly measured. For the purposes of our inquiry (if, indeed, inquiry be needed in matters of common sense, which it usually is not) we have not only to *take into account* general impressions in which it is impossible to have exact measurements, we have to give them the *chief* importance.

Take another example. We are told that with regard to certain documents, notably certain sacred documents, that their unauthenticity has been 'Scientifically' established. A particular case is the Gospel of St. John, or, as those who want to be rid of it are fond of calling it, the Fourth Gospel (the implication being that it was not written by St. John). The so-called 'Scientific' evidence in this case consists of perhaps a dozen main points. You find that its authenticity was denied by one small and obscure heretical set a long time after it was written. You find—or rather it is obvious—that the style is quite different from the style of the other three Gospels. You find that it has phrases in it similar to phrases in Pagan and Jewish work separate from the Christian Scriptures: and you can tabulate a much larger number of points far less important and most of them negligible. You tabulate all these. You note all fragmentary allusions to or quotations from the Gospel in early times, including discrepancies in these allusions. You mix up the certain, the probable, the possible, and what is merely guesswork, into one lump, not distinguishing each part from the other in proportion to credibility, and you call your result—which you set out to prove and to which you strained every particle of evidence—a 'Scientific conclusion.'

It is nothing of the kind. Such a spirit is the very opposite of the scientific spirit. The scientific spirit to begin with asks to see *all* the evidence relative to the issue that can be got. To leave out the overwhelming voice of tradition; to leave out the fact that in a highly-cultured time with constant coming and going throughout the Roman Empire the authorship was taken for granted universally; to leave out all the centuries of unquestioned acceptance; to leave out the absence of contemporary challenge, is no more scientific than it would be to reject all documentary evidence or criticism of manuscripts. And there is more than this: whoever wrote the Gospel of St. John wrote something quite unique. A knowledge of men will convince the reader that whoever wrote that piece of work had the impress of a personality violently driven home. It is not cast in the form of a treatise; it is cast in the form of a narrative, and of a narrative by a witness. You have evidence of all kinds, evidence of the place of origin carried on over not more than two lifetimes, internal evidence that the writer was intimately acquainted with Palestine, and with Palestine before the fall of Jerusalem, internal evidence that he seems to have been so acquainted with it as a young man when the events described were taking place. All that evidence a scientific mind takes into account. It is not scientific to leave out that overwhelming mass of evidence; it is grossly unscientific to do so. Because the one type of evidence is mechanical and qualitative, the other moral and qualitative, does not make the former conclusive and the latter negligible. It is rather the other way about.

I may switch off from that particular and famous instance to another which is in everyone's mouth to-day. I mean the 'Scientific' argument drawn from geology against Christian truth. It is quite admirably unscientific. It nearly always begins by defining as historical Christian doctrine what never was, and never will be, historical Christian doctrine. It goes on by affirming with regard to the unknown past of man, a number of events which are purely imaginary: for instance, a gradual ascension in morals without any sharp and distinctive 'setback.' It proceeds to an affirmation that the Divine Will never intended for man a supernatural state of blessedness, on which geology is about as competent to speak as chemistry is competent to talk about Keats's object in writing 'The Ode to a Nightingale.'

There is no lack of instances. There is the 'Scientific' proof against immortality drawn from experiments on the brain, which teach one not a whit more than has always been known: that if you knocked a man on the head you stunned him, and that if you knocked him on the head hard enough you killed him. There is the 'Scientific' proof against freewill from statistics of criminality and environment: the 'Scientific' proof against the Resurrection which we owe to the mighty pen of Dr. Barnes, who discovered modern chemistry to have proved what nobody had ever suspected before, to wit, that the human body after death corrupts and is dissolved.

I think the moral is simple enough. The moment any of us sees that word 'Scientific,' let him beware. It is a sign-post. It is like one of those big coloured marks they put on roads to warn the motorist that he is approaching the peril of cross-traffic. It is the danger signal bidding us look out for fools.

It ought not to be so, with such a word as Science. It is a noble word, for it originates in that pursuit of truth which is the second noblest of men's activities. Only through misuse has it come to mean, in the mouths of the unintelligent, an increasing blind faith, in the mouths of their superiors, a laughing-stock.

XXVI

On Diaries

IT IS STRANGE THAT A PRACTICE THE MOST SELF-
ISH AND SELF-CENTRED IN THE WORLD SHOULD
be of exceptional value to our fellow-beings. So it
is with Diaries. Take them by and large, they are
of much more value to mankind in general than any
other kind of writing, except the inspired; for they
are usually, in spite of themselves, a witness. Inspired verse, inspired doctrine, inspired morals come
first; but after these Diaries.

It is true that some Diaries or 'journals' (to give
the more general term) are not selfish, for instance
the log of a ship. They are official and necessary,
though even so they are not infrequently tinged
with a personal motive. But the mass of Diaries
are written from one of three motives, or from
parts of these three motives combined; the motive
of recovering one's own past and of giving a sort
of solidity to the fluid passage of life: the motive
of glory (or revenge, which is the same thing) to

make known whom one has met, how great one is, or how offensive was an enemy: and the motive of record, especially in connexion with money.

Now all these motives are personal, highly self-centred, and, in the vast bulk of what is so written, entirely selfish, yet I say that the Diary is of the utmost use to mankind in general. It is useful in defeating the attempts of lawyers to condemn innocent men to death or lesser penalties—though (alas!) it is not equally useful in securing the condemnation of rogues; for rogues cannot be condemned unless those in authority act against them, but with the worst and greatest rogues those in authority are hand in glove. The Diary is of use also in determining disputes other than legal. But the major value of Diaries is undoubtedly their value for history. It is worth while examining closely in what that value consists, because Diaries as historical evidence have been misused, and when they are misused they are worse than useless; they simply pervert history.

It has often been said that history written from official documents must necessarily be ridiculous, because the people who write official documents are actually paid to lie. That is a true saying. Now the Diarist is not paid to lie, but he has all those motives for lying of which I have spoken, vain-glory and revenge. Apart from this fact that Diaries are falsified deliberately by their writers, they are often written up from notes and from memory. They will represent hearsay as experience and talk of general experiences where the writer has nothing but a very local and particular one (thus I have seen this entry in a perfectly genuine and honest Diary written by an Irish Unionist during the late successful rebellion: 'Everyone is expecting the worst and hopes to be able to get away to England in time;' here 'everyone' can hardly be meant for the whole Irish people, but must mean the writer's own small circle).

Diaries are, then, untrustworthy as direct evidence, if you read their general expressions too literally, or if you do not allow for the emotions or isolation of the writer—and particularly for the various human vices of boasting, falsehood, spite, and all the rest of the charming train. But they are of overwhelming importance as indirect evidence—and for this quality in them I will bless and praise the name of every Diarist, however vile, untrustworthy or muddle-headed, that was ever pupped.

Thus I have recently been re-reading Evelyn for the purposes of history, and I also have been looking into Pepys (very few people read him through, and I don't pretend to have done so). Pepys is a much honester man than Evelyn, for Evelyn had a lot of the Puritan about him. But allow for the other man who thinks that the Puritan is a noble fellow and that debauchery is worse than covetousness and hypocrisy. He will say that Pepys is the wicked man and Evelyn the good man. No matter —the point is that each Diarist informs you, not so much by saying what he feels himself, but by allusions which are unconscious. Thus when Evelyn going through the town casually remarks a woman being burnt in Smithfield for murdering her husband, and then goes on to other more important matters, it is illuminating to the modern reader, because it throws a light upon the state of mind at the time. Evelyn thought of the burning of a woman at Smithfield, more than a century after Mary Tudor and some years before the condemnation of Alice Lisle (she, by the way, was only beheaded, though condemned to be burnt), as a pitiful but ordinary event; much as we may regard a Black Maria taking men to penal servitude. That explains to the historian why they went on burning women here up to the French Revolution.

Or again, when Pepys tells us that he asks the serving maid to come up and sing with him and his wife (in a Catch or Glee, if I remember right), it is a startling commentary upon the difference between that day and ours. He thought of a domestic as a companion just like himself, only poorer and subject to all manner of pressure and worry, as a child is. He never thought of the less fortunate as a separate sort of human being. If Pepys had written this by way of affectation, to show how noble he was, regarding all human beings as equals, it would be worthless as evidence of the social morals of his time. Putting it as he does, clearly, without affectation and as a matter of course, it is invaluable evidence.

Though they have obviously been touched up out of all knowing, there is some value in Sidney's Diary and Reresby's, not for what they express as opinions, nor even for that to which they bear witness as supporting their opinions—all that is propaganda—but as unconscious evidence of the way in which the men of their own time carried on.

I ask myself sometimes whether our modern Diarists will have any such value for posterity. At the first reading I am inclined to doubt it. They are so outrageously false that they would seem to have no value at all. Nearly all the modern Diaries I have read are clearly written to serve the writer's individual purpose without scruple; a purpose generally of vanity, and always quite particular to him or to her self. Moreover, they lie quite outrageously, trusting (and in this they are justified) to the inability of the reply catching up with the original falsehood. The reply would, at the best, be a short letter in small type hidden away behind the mass of a newspaper, and at the worst and commonest will not be published at all. I have myself read in modern Diaries a good score of such allusions to words put into my own mouth which I not only never uttered, but which I could not have uttered because I was not present at the time; and that experience I am sure is familiar to hosts of others in this Cads' Concert of Dreadful Revelations, Secret Histories, and Liftings of the Social Veil from which we have suffered so terribly since the War. Further, our modern Diaries (I am talking of English ones) though they can say ridiculous or abusive things about individuals, cannot give important news about public life because such commentary is forbidden under heavy penalties—perhaps to the advantage of the State.

Nevertheless, I believe that even these modern Diaries, yes, even those inexcusable ones published within the very lifetime of the Diarist, have a certain historical value. For whether the liar means to do it or no, he cannot help telling the truth upon things which seem to him insignificant, but which may be of the highest value to the chronicler some centuries hence. For instance, I read in one such a short time ago an account of a dinner, which the wretched author said he had attended, and perhaps had. To my personal and certain knowledge a conversation he described there never took place. To my personal and certain knowledge he represented himself as an important guest in a gathering where . he was hardly noticed. But, in that passage, he alludes to a couple of blocks in the traffic, so bad that it took him a quarter of an hour in a cab to go not much more than half a mile between the end of Mayfair and the beginning of Westminster. Now I take it to be conceivable, or even probable, that a posterity not very remote will have lost all memory of our present traffic conditions in London. These may be, as let us hope they are, ephemeral. The bulk of what will be our classical literature of the nineteenth and early twentieth century knew nothing of such congestion. But, what an illuminating point for a future historian!

Or again, when the future historian is wondering why the railway was divided into first and third class, what an eye-opener to come on this one phrase, 'It was one of the old second-class carriages transformed'—even though that phrase came in the midst of hopeless falsehood. Or again (to quote another real phrase which I read but the other day in one of these books), 'She can't afford to send her son to Eton, so she is sending him to Shrewsbury.'

But this, as the Bishop said, would take me far.

XXVII

On Pavement Artists

O F ALL THE ARTISTS OF MY TIME, I LOVE THE PAVEMENT ARTIST BEST. HE SEEMS TO ME TO have the qualities that the artists had in the greatest day of art. He depends frankly upon patronage; he is indifferent to fame; he does not even sign. He is in love with his work; it is beautiful to see the care and interest with which he will work up his effect. He is strongly bound by tradition, which is the very sustenance of all good art; he exercises himself upon conventional subjects, and those subjects are of a sort that appeal to the mass of his fellowmen. He seems to be free from envy, and he keeps himself remote from the flattery of the rich; he belongs to no clique; he uses no jargon. He begins at the beginning, proceeding by the right sort of procession, a deviation from which gets all art wrong; that is, he begins by trying to represent the thing which he pictures, whether it be an apple, a sunset, a boat in a storm, or the Monarch. His colours are

228

the true colours which we all have in mind. His skies are blue, except those at evening, when they are red; his grass is green, and the foam of his waves is white. He has a strong grasp of the eternal principle that the work of a man must be carried out within limitations; he puts a frame round all he does; and he begins with an outline. He very rightly appeals to the emotions, and, still more rightly, he is happiest when he feels that his picture tells a story. He makes no attempt to startle, trouble or offend the middle classes, and depends on their patronage. He lies, as a man should lie, simply, humbly, and for profit; and, like all good men, he prefers acting a lie to speaking one. That is why he always takes the pennies out of the hat the moment they are put in, so that the charitable shall imagine that he has taken nothing all day.

Even among pavement artists I have my favourites, though they are all excellent. There is one close to where I live. I pass him every morning on my way into town. Properly speaking, he is not a single artist, but a syndicate; for though it is clear that the pictures are all by the same hand, yet different men appear upon different days to receive the reward of talent. I can well believe that there is enough to support four or five families, for I live in a neighbourhood where men are rich enough to give, but not rich enough to be avaricious. I notice with pleasure that there is anxiety in his (or rather their) mind about the importance of keeping up one's prices. Nothing is refused. He would not tear up —they would not tear up—an insufficient cheque and send it back in morsels to the donor. You might make the cheque as small as you liked—I am certain he would take it. Some day I shall try the experiment.

All artistic work is precarious to-day. Modern taste changes bewilderingly, for the simple reason that men believe a thing to be beautiful on authority nowadays—being quite unable to tell beauty for themselves. Not only does taste change, but the type of market changes. Only half a lifetime ago the market for furnishing the walls of the newly-rich with landscape was brisk; to-day it is dead. To-day one must either draw advertisements, fine ladies, or politicians, to make a livelihood. Pigments fade. Whole groups of manner in painting become old-fashioned and ridiculous. I say it is always a precarious trade. But it is less precarious with the pavement artist than it is with his more stuck-up brother of the studio. There is only one thing that he worries about, and that is the weather.

On a really wet day he cannot transfer nature through his medium, because his medium runs. He cannot express his reactions to the world through the vehicle of his art, because in wet weather the vehicle won't work.

I knew one of this great company who tried to outflank the trouble by drawing his pictures on glazed paper, leaning them up against a wall where there was cover above. But his gallant effort failed, for two reasons: first, that the public found him unconventional—he was not doing what they expected, so they passed him by; next, that men are not generous in the rain. They watch the weather, therefore, with more care than modern sailors, do these most sincere and downright of our æsthetic world. Note carefully, you will find that a wet morning does not drive them away. They mark the very moments when the stones are dry enough for the colours to take, and they are back at their haunts.

Though these men lack the vices of their craft, and can boast a much higher place in morals, as they also can, I think, in sense of beauty and in the right philosophy of creation, than to any of which their not wealthier, but prouder, rivals can claim, yet they have one thing in common with almost every man or woman that ever fiddled about with clay or turpentine; and that is, an eagerness to let the public know something about themselves. They publish no memoirs; they are too decent to talk about other people; but they set, right beside their own works, and in the same medium, some simple statement of their right to attention. Sometimes they tell us that the work is wholly their own; sometimes they are married and have a family; sometimes that they have been wounded; sometimes that they have no other means of support. I should like to see this custom spread throughout the whole profession. I should like to see a Cubist putting down in crimson on the left-hand corner of his canvas, 'The best I can do'; or someone who has painted a wealthy woman in the chocolate-box manner write underneath, 'Entirely my own unaided work.' What, I think, would be better still, would be for those horrible modern parasites who pass before us as newly-discovered geniuses every few weeks to set down in bold, square lettering, 'A lawfully married man with six children.' No one would believe him unless he gave an address out of Chelsea. But it would be a tribute to decent morals, at any rate; and that is something damnably needed in this our time.

Talking of which, I marvel that fashionable artists do not advertise. There is no professional rule against it, as there is with doctors. They know very well what reviews are read by the wealthy, and a particularly good field would be the New York weekly press, especially of the highbrow sort. 'Mr. Phillip Cobble, has painted two Duchesses and one Shareshuffler. He can also do animals, and he makes the dogs look like human beings. He will be happy to send reduced specimens of his work done in the three-colour process.'

The first man to do this sort of thing would get nothing but contempt, but if it took on and there was competition, I am sure it would pay. Better still would it be to take a whole page and print a fairly good reproduction in colour of some portrait one had done, showing an extremely wicked man with a benign, intelligent, but firm face, and dressed, as portraits usually are, expensively. Then the New York people who were just going over to Europe in boats would bear it in mind, and some one of them would be almost certain to bite.

But as I write a quantity of ideas swarm upon me. For instance, 'I forge Corot,' with a box-number address, and specimens to be had on applying. There is no trade in the world where illustration would have more effect. It is all very well for the man who advertises collars or whisky to represent the people wearing and drinking the same as demigods; that may slightly influence, but it does not convince. But actual reproduction of sculpture or painting or drawing is the thing itself. When a man has done a good bust, for instance, let him present a lot of little signed and addressed replicas three or four inches high to hotels for paper weights and match scratchers. . . . But all this is taking me away from pavement artists. So now I shall leave this and go into the street and renew my soul by watching the next one I can find.

XXVIII

On Bridges

O F ALL STRUCTURES WHICH MAN HAS MADE
TO SATISFY HIS NEEDS THE BRIDGE IS THAT IN
which he has been æsthetically most successful, and,
perhaps, structurally least.

From the beginning of recorded history, you have
in long succession the tale of bridges breaking down
and swept away, till the accident becomes a commonplace compared with the failure of other structures.
You have further a limit to effort, very clearly
marked; the effort to obtain height or majesty
through width or length of unbroken emptiness in
other forms of structure, has been an effort successfully progressive and often rapidly progressive. But
bridges, even for the overcoming of comparatively
small obstacles, were felt to be a special triumph.
There was a temptation to make them do more than
the art of the time allowed. One can point to a score
of places in Western Europe (Avignon is the most
famous) where the effort was vanquished, and to

hundreds where what looks to-day like the surmounting of but a trifling span or height was looked on as a marvel, and carries to this day some nickname connoting astonishment.

Meanwhile, structurally perilous, the bridge continued to be, throughout all these centuries preceding our own industrial time, æsthetically a success. It was never offensive; it was usually beautiful, it was sometimes triumphantly beautiful. In this it led every other form of structure. Not, indeed, that others were not greater because more complex achievements of art, but that the bridge offered less exceptions to beauty, or rather, I think, none. I can recollect no bridge dating from before, say 1750, or somewhat later, in Western Europe, that does not satisfy the eye; and I could quote fifty off-hand which are masterpieces.

To-day the position is exactly reversed. The bridging of spans which our fathers would have thought insurmountable to man, the carrying of a way for wheels or water at a height which they would have thought equally insurmountable, have become commonplace. Meanwhile, of all our æsthetic failures, the failure of the bridge is the most glaring—and it is getting worse. With the coming of concrete there threatens the peril that the bridge may become *normally* the ugly and even offensive structure which iron had already begun to make it.

It is worth while going into this contrast and seeing if we can discover its causes, in the hope of finding some remedy. It will not be easy to find those causes; it will be impossible to discover the most fundamental of them; but some few become apparent upon analysis and may aid us a little in the task.

The reason that the bridge has in the past been structurally given to failure is fairly clear. It proceeds directly from the nature of the function which the bridge has to supply. The function of the bridge is to give man an artificial way over gaps (that is, over obstacles naturally insurmountable without artifice) in his progress from one point to another. Deep water, a strong stream, a profound gulf, the sudden transference of a shelf in a gorge from one bank of the torrent to another, these created the necessity for a bridge. Now the scale upon which these things are bound has no relation to man. A man builds his house or his wall or his fortification in relation to himself; to the scale upon which he is made or upon which are made the instruments of his own creation. But in the case of the bridge he is tempted to attain and if possible surpass a maximum.

There stands between the city and its nearest port a rift. To carry a way across that rift may be manifestly impossible to the means available at a particular time. Thus the seventeenth century could manifestly never have bridged the Menai Straits with any permanent structure. But between what is easily to be done at any one time, and what is manifestly impossible, there is a continuous broken series of natural challenges to man, and the bridge-builder will and must stretch his effort to the limit—and a little beyond. He is not bound to build a tower to a height which his art does not want, nor to impose a weight of wall upon a foundation insufficient for it. But he is bound to do his utmost to overcome the obstacles breaking a continuous and necessary road, and only under compulsion will man admit that the limit to his effort as a bridge-builder has been passed in any particular instance. He will set you a pile bridge of lashed timber across a violent current. He will strain material to its utmost in the overcoming of some very great span. He will always have examples in any period of the bridge coming up to the perilous limit of safety and beyond it.

That, of course, is as true to-day as it was in the

most primitive times. We have our bridge disasters
to-day with our latest materials—as across the St.
Lawrence, or, a lifetime ago, across the estuary of
the Tay; or upon the girder bridge across the Loire
just after the War. But the contrast exists in the fact
that we have not yet, in most places, challenged our
limits. The advance of mechanical power and of the
adaptation of material have gone so much faster than
our needs that we have not yet reached the stage of
commonly attempting the extreme limits of our
power. Further, modern society, with its numerous
and complex regulations and its highly-policed industrialism, imposes a margin of safety which is, as
a rule, jealously observed. There is, therefore, a
very real contrast here between the new industrial
world and all the older centuries. The modern
bridge is structurally a success, and even a triumph.
You may stand under the gossamer arch which spans
the upper valley of (I think) the Lot (or one of
those mountain tributaries of the Dordogne) and
marvel how man could have thrown that light web
of steel across such a waste of air.

Even with the older materials we can do what our
fathers could never have done. I may instance that
superb stone bridge at Luxemburg, carried in a single
span (either the largest or the second largest in the

world) from one rock to the other, above the chasm which had for centuries protected that natural fortress. Here modern engineering has been able to do what our ancestors could never have done, though it was using the oldest of materials. It was able to do so because modern engineering possessed the implements for constructing the huge centring of the thing, and for hanging out far over the edge of the gulf, and putting exactly in its place, each great stone of the ellipse. I am told that in this particular case the pressure was so great that mortar could not be used, and that plates of lead were put in for a binding between the stones.

The ancients did, indeed, carry ways, especially for water, over heights and across distances as great; but they could only do it by a multiplicity of arches and of tiers, such as remain to us in the great aqueduct of Segovia or in the Pont du Gard or in the ruins of Cherchell. We can do the thing on a new scale altogether.

We can also do it in new ways. The tubular bridge was a new way (and a hideous one); the suspension bridge, though not a new way, was new in the scale upon which it was applied, and in the material which made that scale possible; it was also more tolerable to the eye than most of the new methods. The girder bridge was new, of whatever section, and now we have the beginning of the concrete bridge, such as the famous one at Pasadena or the great monster over the Rhine, which you pass going north from Mayence.

So much for the contrast in facility (and, I think, one may fairly say, in safety), as also for the contrast in scale—in which last point we shall very likely add such new achievements as will make even the greatest of our existing bridges small in comparison with their successors.

What of the contrast in beauty?

Before going into that, there is a point to be noted which has been emphasised again and again in our time, but never seems to have been fully appreciated. That point is, the *necessity* of beauty for man. If what you make, especially what you make to be permanent, is offensive, it is, in the degree of its ugliness, *a true economic loss*. It is just as much a failure to build an ugly house as it is to build a leaky house, or a house that tumbles down; and if you neglect the positive need which mankind has for beauty, you are neglecting an element as vital to the State as any of the more easily measurable elements upon which you may have concentrated.

Why was the old bridge nearly always beautiful,

or at least satisfying, and often supremely lovely, although other structures of the same period might be indifferent?

I say again that a complete answer is certainly not to be discovered, but I can offer a few tentative suggestions.

In the first place the bridge more than almost any other structure depended upon local material, because it needed a special effort upon a considerable scale. Local material is generally consonant with the landscape in which it is fashioned. But that is a small point. More important as a cause of beauty was, I think, the fact that the very use of the bridge involved beautiful lines and justly proportioned spaces. The level bridge had to satisfy the eye on proportions of its spans, because it had to satisfy the traveller's feeling for safety in a material which he himself understood and with which he was familiar. The arch, when it was the plain round arch, could never go wrong; and when the Renaissance developed the elliptical arch it fell upon a curve which also satisfied the sense of proportion. The catenary curve of the suspension cable, primitive or late, is in the same category.

Another cause, as it seems to me, lies in the combination of effort and simplicity. The building of a bridge was always a considerable affair, and at the same time its functions as a carrier so much overwhelmed decorative motive, that there was little chance for the latter to run wild or to go astray.

I am not quite sure that the fact of a bridge being a public thing did not contribute here. Nor that a public thing tends to be more beautiful than a private one; it is rather the other way with many objects. But a thing of wide public use lends itself less (save in times like our own, when the populace have ceased to have any effective control) to extravagance and falsity in detail.

Lastly, the bridge was essentially traditional. It had begun as a difficult thing; the art of constructing it had achieved a few main rules, and the sense of peril forbade them to be departed from. Now tradition is, as we all know, the great safeguard of beauty.

There are much deeper causes than these, of course; beauty springs from sources more profound than these material circumstances, and our own loss of beauty to-day is rather a loss of some spiritual value than a thing imposed upon us by our implements. Still, for what they are worth, I suggest these few causes of the beauty of bridges among all other structures. And they were not only beautiful as individual structures; they were beautiful in their grouping and their position. Of their nature they could be seen by many at large from far below or from far away and in a hundred aspects; that tempted the good builder to a proper use of site. Everyone will agree, I think, that the best stonework of our last century—I mean Waterloo Bridge—is inspired by and marries with the tidal Thames; and everyone will agree that the lofty bridge which introduces the pilgrim to Toledo is in the spirit of the Tagus gorge, and the savage sweep it makes around Toledo Hill. But what are the corresponding causes in our failure in this matter since the modern industrial advantage began?

One answer commonly given has always seemed to me very doubtful. It is this: that we have a hereditary acquaintance with stone, brick and wood, so that the introduction of a new material—iron and steel, concrete, and whatever may come next—leaves us without a standard. The new stuff is ungrateful to us because we have no ancestral memory of it, or have not yet developed an æsthetic understanding of it.

The reason that answer seems to me false is that man in older times, using a new material, has not used it hideously. The savage who has never seen

244

iron till he could get a bit of it by bartering with the white man, will fashion that iron beautifully; and the first use of stone by a people long living in places where stone was unknown, the first use of the imported material, does not, in any instance I can recall, begin repulsively and gradually acquire beauty.

Another answer which I also think false is this: the answer that steel and concrete and new materials in general, are ill-used æsthetically, because we attempt to give them beauty through methods of decoration and of general line derived from other and older materials; because we have not yet developed or hit upon a line and decoration proper to themselves.

This seems to me a false answer, because man did undoubtedly continue, always, the influence of an older material upon a newer one; and he has always done so with success, because he was acting naturally and rightly in so doing. The Greek stone-work reproduces the beam and the wooden trunk and the flat-sloping wooden roof of its climate, and is all the better for doing so. The Mongol roof-lines reproduce the tent.

Nor is the right answer exactly to be found in the complaint that the modern builder is indifferent to beauty. He often attempts to achieve it, and yet in the new material almost invariably fails.

I think that at least a suggestion in the matter may be made—very incomplete, I know—when I say that our worst handicap is the false doctrine inherited from the æsthetic philosophy of the nineteenth century (and especially repeated in this country) that beauty, and the decorative extremes of it, depend upon the general function of material; that the eye is satisfied essentially because it sees something useful, and consonant to the material used. Ruskin abounded in this sense, and he was only one of a herd in his philosophy, though he was unique in his command of rhythmical prose. I conceive that doctrine to be false, and I think that when we shall have got well rid of it and be ready to decorate with what we know or feel to be beautiful in shape and relief, be ready to give variety of line by any method which satisfies our eye, we shall then be able to deal with the new material as successfully as the men of our blood did with the old.

What has the fluting of a Greek pillar to do with structure? In what way is a Greek sculptured garland of leaves and fruits and banded linen consonant with stone? Those who achieved beauty in the past did so through the action of three forces at work in them: a sense of proportion, the nurture of tradition, and a necessity for satisfying the eye. Tradition in the new materials we have not; but tradition in decoration and of detail we can recover. And as for the other two, they are in every man, or at any rate in normal man, when his life is sanely and normally lived.

For, indeed, life lived insanely and abnormally as it is to-day in our industrial civilisation, would and does produce monstrosity in oak or marble just as much as in massed concrete or in steel.

XXIX

On Not Reading Books

IT IS NOW EXACTLY SEVENTEEN YEARS AGO THAT
I BEGAN A BALLADE OF WHICH THE REFRAIN
was the line:

> Heaven help us all, the books I ought to read!

I forget whether I finished that ballade or not.
I fancy I did. Some day I shall find it somewhere
in my stock of unpublished stuff, drag it out, and
sell it for a prodigious sum to the English, the Scotch,
the Welsh and the peoples of the New World; but
not, indeed, to those unacquainted with the tongue
in which it is written. Perhaps, on the other hand,
I never finished it, in which case (by the Dog!) I
never shall.

I remember the *envoi* now; it ran like this:

> Prince, either you or someone in your name
>> Wrote some remarks upon the Hampshire breed
> Of hogs. I haven't read it. All the same—
>> Heaven help us all, the books I ought to read!

248

I write these remarks, not in pride, nor in anger, nor even in imbecility, but from humility. I am perpetually wishing that I could read more, and to be honest, I read nothing. At least, I read nothing of my contemporaries. When I do I find them fairly good. They put me to shame. They have the most marvellous adventures, especially in the way of paper love. They can get right into the souls of people who do not interest me—but even that is an achievement. They can make guesses at things of which they know nothing, in anthropology, geology, morphology and all the ologies except teleology; and (of course) theology (of that in a moment—be patient). Then they can write new guesses upsetting the old ones, and then new guesses again, and each of these guesses is put forward as a final dogma. I know I ought to read them, but I don't.

I confess to a very sincere admiration of my friends who review novels. I know, quite intimately, at least five men who review novels (if I may say so respectfully) in the bulk; as men scrape fish in a fish shop.

They themselves deal with twenty novels a week. And I have heard that there is one firm of publishers in London which produces three novels a day. I take it (I have not read them) that each of these novels turns upon the attraction (and repulsion) of the sexes one for the other. As there are only two sexes I should have thought the theme was getting thin; but I must be wrong—for the spate goes on.

Now I say it sincerely; I have an immense admiration—more than an immense admiration, a bewildered and sudden admiration—for the men who review these things. I cannot do it, because there has been put into my mind either by my Creator or by some little Dæmon, a sort of catch which jabs up and stops me reading after the first two or three lines. Indeed, when I do read a book (alas for me!) it is nearly always because I open it at random in the middle and find something that strikes me. But the beginning always knocks me out. When I read a beginning like this: 'It was already dark and she was waiting,' my mind gives way and I go back to some of the more simple problems of arithmetic or to a cross-word puzzle. When I read, 'John Henderson had for fourteen years sat upon his stool in the bank,' I stop at once like a little ship striking the bar as it tries to get into harbour. A shock runs through me and I see that it is all up.

Or, again, 'There is no more beautiful spot in Europe than La Tour de Force which stands under the height. . . .' My mortal soul utters a groan, and there is nothing doing. In this way I miss the masterpieces of our time.

Since the fashion is for public confession let me go further and fare worse. When a book is widely advertised, at great expense to the kindly publisher who has undertaken to publish it, the mere advertisement destroys in me all power of reading it. If I am told that it deals with my contemporaries— why, I know my contemporaries so well that I cannot conceive any interest in them. If it deals with the past, why I know the past so little that I shirk the adventure.

Now in this line of confession let me confess again. If any book deal with a journey to the planets, no matter how badly it be written, no matter what a goat the writer may be, what abominable sentiment he breaks into during his narration, no matter what the padding of pseudo-science, no matter what the strange style, I am on. I am afraid I have missed a few, but I honestly believe I have read more than half of those that have appeared in the English tongue during the last thirty years. And as with the planets, so with Atlantis. I can eat Atlantis. No man can give me enough of Atlantis. One of my great regrets is that there are not enough places left in the world for imaginary adventures.

There was one admirable book I remember years ago, called *Ninety North*—that was before the North Pole was discovered. I have read it at least fifteen times. I have read 'Dr. Nikola's' Adventures on the Upper Brahmaputra (lovely word!) quite six times, and perhaps seven. And if anyone will write me a book about some really unknown place (I suggest South London) I am on. Save for that large category of Romance I am afraid I have no wide field open to me.

What, then, do people do who, like me, have this abominable weakness in literary appetite? I tell you, they read the same books over and over again. That reminds me that I have left out one category, books about the Other World. Why the Other World is put in the singular I do not know. I should say at a guess it was a good deal more multiple than this world, which is saying a good deal. Anyhow, I will read books on the Other World; as, for instance, I will read over and over again a book called *The Outer Darkness*, which is all about the Queen of Hell—a Peach, if ever there was one! But the books about the Other World are all too few—yet what an immense area for expansion! We all know even less about it than we do about pre-history, which is fascinating in its way. But, talking of

pre-history, I do wish people would write honest
romances about it, like *La Guerre du Feu,* or that
delightful book *Realmah,* a true gentleman's book
and no nonsense about it; it is by the author of
Friends in Council. Who reads either of them now?
Both jolly good books!

But I digress, or rather I am lost in a jumble
and mess from which I cannot escape. Farewell,
then, to you, all you book readers! Continue to
read books and may they profit you! I envy you.
I admire you! I know that I cannot compete with
you—and I will not put my signature to this nonsense without recommending to all living men (I
am afraid it is no good recommending it to the
women) that book called *The Worm Ouroboros.*
It is the romance of a world that never was, not
even of the Other World. Its landscapes are magnificent. One lives in it. I read it by fits and starts
in the year 1923, beginning at Torquay, continuing
throughout a night anchored outside Lyme Regis,
again in an evening, abominably anchored in Chesil
Cove, where the horses are fed upon human flesh
and men wear ear-rings. I did not read it going
through Portland Race, for anyone who can read
anything going through Portland Race must either
be a God or a Beast, but I read it running along the

Dorset coast in the most glorious weather. I read it again at the end of that little passage in the secure haven of Hamble River, where I completed my reading. And that's that.

P.S.—I am about to read Le Dornec on Atheism. I do not know which side he takes.

XXX

On Advertisement

(WITH SOME, BUT LITTLE, RELATION TO
CHRISTMAS)

TIME WAS WHEN CHRISTMAS CARDS DEALT WITH
THE NATIVITY. THAT SMALL AFFAIR WAS
ousted out in my early manhood; so no more of it.

Time was when any man writing upon Christmas
had to write more or less in connexion with the
Feast. Such superstition gave way to a more general
talk of Peace and Goodwill. Peace, anyhow, to
anybody; and Goodwill at large. We must conform
to our environment or perish (at least, so I am as-
sured), and it is clear that anything connected with
Christmas to-day should also be connected with advertisement.

Now to advertise Christmas would obviously be
a waste of energy—which is another way of saying
a waste of money. For in the first place you cannot
sell Christmas, and in the second place everybody

knows the date—though most people have almost forgotten its meaning. So let me write, in the pleasant soothing manner proper to the Season, of Peace to swindlers and Goodwill to scoundrels, of advertisement in general; of Publicity; of how pleasant it is, how just, of what value to our culture and of its glorious future. Whether I shall have a space to get to the Glorious Future before I have done with the disquisition I doubt; but, at any rate, I will meander through the other chapters of my sermon.

Well, the things I notice most about advertisements in this Holy Season (as in all others) is the health and regular features of the people who live in that world. It is not my world, nor, I fear, is it yours. It is a world not of this world. It is inhabited by few people, consumers and producers; now of these, I say, the consumers of the goods advertised are remarkable for their health and their regularity of feature. Note; I do not call it their beauty.

'Twas but yestere'en (I beg your pardon) that I saw an advertisement of a young man giving the *Encyclopædia Britannica* (of all God's creatures!) to a lady, whom I presume and hope was his wife. It is true that the word 'wife' means little nowadays; but I carry the prejudices of my youth. At any rate, he is giving it to a young woman. A slight, fixed smile is on his face; the smile that befits the doer of good deeds. On hers there is an expression of as much ecstasy as can be pumped up in a semi-detached villa; she is clasping her hands convulsively (so strong is her emotion), and her eyes, though expressed only by dots, register Immediate Beatitude.

I am not concerned with whether she be wise or unwise in thus finding the end of her being and the sum of all delights in the umpteenth edition of the *Encyclopædia Britannica*, but rather with the regularity of her features and his. They would be more human, these young people, if they had more of a twist about their mouths and eye-lines, but they have not—and I let it go at that. There is another type of consumer—they call it in America the 'College Boy'—who is depicted wearing collars, drawers and vests, waterproofs, hats, and I don't know what else, but always with the same amazing lack of individual energy, always with the same amazing lack of suffering, profundity, knowledge, expectation, irony, desire, and the stuff of life. His wooden head is regular, always and everywhere.

I add to my gallery the Aged Colonel with the complexion of thirty and the hair of eighty-five, and the Elderly (not aged) City Man. The Aged

Colonel shoots with a gun; the Elderly City Man puts on evening clothes and either sips wine (or, what is much worse, whisky) or smokes something. Sometimes he is saying kind things about a shaving soap, at other times he is recommending a polish. But one thing he always is—dead, from the neck up; pure bone. The regularity of his features is my despair. What! O last heir of a fallen race! Have you never felt remorse? Have you never known anxiety? Have you never yearned, let alone loved? Have you not lost so much as a piece of money in the street and failed to find it after grubbing in the mud? Have you never even missed a train? His features answer me he has never experienced any of these things which we experience; and as for the awful doom of human kind, he knows no more of it than a cow.

So much for the consumers. What of the producers?

There, for some extraordinary reason, the rule is reversed; everything turns right-about-face. The advertisers represent the producers of soaps, collars, cigarettes, in a gallery of the most inexcusable villains imaginable—men much worse than the real bad men whom I have met in my life (and Heaven knows I have met a fine selection of them). Their features are lined with every kind of violence, cunning; their deliberate reticence for the purpose of overreaching their neighbours, the falsehood of their thin lips, the cruelty of their flashing eyes, their dark oily hair, disgust the observer, their mean, brilliant glances affect him as he might be affected by some tropical animal.

I have sometimes desired to get through the paper and the paste and to wander in that world. I have desired to meet the College Boy, the Young Suburban Bride, the Aged Colonel, the Elderly City Man. I have thought it might be a diversion to spend a day or two among the bone-heads. They all of them have plenty of money, they are all cheerful, they are all well. There is no poverty among them, nor any parting, nor disappointment, nor deception—save, indeed, in the one case of the man who goes mad with rage because he has not got the kind of petrol he wants—though God knows he cannot tell petrol by the label on the tin. They pay no income-tax. They do not know the difference between good wine and bad. They believe what they read—if, indeed, they can read—and they smile and smile. Theirs must be a soothing world.

I would answer them exactly according to their minds. I would say the most abominable things of

poor men on strike for decent wages, or—if it is getting a little late for that—of any other Aunt Sally
of the papers. I will admit that we were not given
to boasting, that we were in all essential respects the
salt of the earth. I would take an interest in foot-
ball, golf, and the awful peril of a Socialist Government, headed by Mr. MacDonald and Mr. Snow-
den, old Uncle Tom Cobley, or anybody else. I
would pretend that the Dominions were simply parts
of England, and that the people and landscape of
the United States were indistinguishable from those
of Devonshire. I would congratulate them on the
termination of the lock-out, or whatever new little
affair might be on in the industrial world when I
should have the honour to be admitted to their company. I should show them that there was a good
time coming. I should quote the highly original
public speeches of all Royalties. I should even
denounce poor old William Hohenzollern, and, of
course, the Moscow clique—whom I should be careful to call 'Russians.' Oh! believe me! I should get
on with the fool world of consumers in the advertisements admirably well, and I should especially be
careful to tell all the dumb wenches that they must
be careful to keep their complexions.

I would discuss the great writers of our time, confining my speech again to the women, because the men do not read; and when I say great writers, I mean, of course, novelists and dramatists, for I am quite sure that among the guys on the posters, no other kind of writing counts. I should be hard on trade unions—but admit their legitimate function. I should say nothing about the power of the banks. I should call all lawyers impeccable, but especially the failures who had been shelved on the Bench.

I think I should get on with the producers too, saluting them as fellow-villains, digging them in the ribs, winking and suggesting all manner of tricks whereby they could further bamboozle, swindle and defraud their fellow-men.

*   *   *   *   *

And yet, I am afraid I should get tired of that world very soon. For its crudity and enormity of contrasts and its lack of nuance would fatigue me. Even as it is they fatigue me. I would give worlds to repose my eyes upon some pictured seller a little less villainous, some buyer a little less abjectly crass.

It is right that the consumer should be made out a fool, for a fool he is. It is right that the man who takes in the fool should be represented as a villain, for a villain he must naturally be—or try to be.   But why upon this scale, why in this excess, why with this crude emphasis?

I have no doubt that the experienced producers in these matters would tell one that any variation of type would spell disastrous loss.   It may be so. If that be their reason for drawing such people in such a fashion, they have my benediction.   Anything which makes money for them or for anybody else is sacred.

But for my part, if ever a higher artist should arise who shall put into any advertisement any human being with some little complexity of life, and some little character about him, I might possibly do what I have never yet done in my life, and that is, spend a few pence upon the wares so advertised.

XXXI

On Certain Terms

IT IS A FALSE CRITICISM OF THE ENGLISH LAN-
GUAGE TO BE PERPETUALLY INSISTING UPON
exactitude in sense, let alone exactitude in spelling.
The English language is the product of a quality
unique in Europe, which is a sort of excess (if that
be possible) in creative imagination, the peculiar
virtue of these islands. I say 'these islands' because
it is to be discovered in Scotland as much as in England, in Wales and (if the Irish will pardon my
including them) in Ireland.

There is in the legend, as in the fiction, in the
solemn religious dogmatic utterances, as in the
vaguest emotional expression, which have proceeded
from these ocean peoples, a vividness in the visualisa-
tion of people and things and phantasms of the mind
which would seem to have no equal of which we
are in Europe aware. The characters of fiction are
intensely individual, like living men and women, not

263

types; the vision of landscapes might be called supernatural; in everything this quality appears.

A language tardily formed under such influences (I say 'tardily,' for it was not in full being until the fifteenth century) must not ask for precision; it can give you magic and the fire of life, and opens windows on to things beyond the world. If it not only can, but must do this, then of its nature it will fail in precision. You will find in it a mass of synonyms and pseudo-synonyms. You will find a more rapid flux in the meaning of the same word, from one generation to another, than you will, I suppose, in other languages. On account of this, I say we ought not to attempt an extreme of precision. It is not in the genius of the tongue.

Nevertheless, there has appeared in the present day a lack of precision which is not native to the tongue or to the spirit which produced that tongue. It arises from a corruption in social life from the pressure of alien societies over which the English language has spread, or by which the English language has been inherited through the enormous venture of the Scotch, the Welsh, the English and the Irish, and their dispersion throughout the world. It arises also from that miserable modern habit of urban life which reduces human society to a dust which kills individual reaction and imposes fashions against what should be the will of individuals, and against what should be the tradition of the corporate body. The main agent of this corruption is the popular daily newspaper, owned by some worthless fellow and produced in a hurry and in fear by his servants.

Under that process a number of valuable terms essential to thought, and, till recently, full of meat and meaning, are being washed down into nothingness like food cooked over and over again and steeped in the water of the cooking. Other terms are being degraded in meaning, given a new sense, precise enough but not less sufficient than the old.

Consider the word 'cynic,' and its derivatives 'cynical' and 'cynicism.' It would be academic and silly to tie down that word to its Greek derivation, which is simply 'doglike.' According to that, a 'cynic' would be a person who wagged his tail, barked and got in the way of motor cars (which, alas! too few cynics manage to do, and too many dogs). But the Greeks applied it to a set of philosophers who denied convention and even morals. Then it came to mean a man who, being accused of a shameful action, boasted himself indifferent to blame; a man who despised and neglected morals.

It is a very powerful word, powerfully condemning something which is a dissolvent of human society, and an enemy thereof; something which it is our business to combat, as we combat any poison. One ought to be able to say, as our fathers said, 'That is cynical,' meaning 'that is abominable.' It ought to connote indignation against the abandonment of the soul's duty to maintain rules of right living.

Now observe what the popular Press has done with that word. It has obliterated the just meaning and put nothing in its place. It has attached to the word 'cynic' the meaning 'one who is the exact opposite of a cynic,' to wit, a man who is indignant against evil, notes it, dwells upon it, and protests against it. A man is called 'cynical' to-day if he emphasises the degree in which his fellow-men are falling away from goodness, if he points out corruption in the State, cruelty and hypocrisy in individuals, exposes self-deception (or, rather, the attempt at it, for real self-deception is impossible to sane men), if he traces the motives of avarice, selfishness and cowardice, he will be called a 'cynic.'

'The cynic,' the writer hurriedly writes, 'would tell us that the mainspring of commercial activity is covetousness.' Or, again, 'Mr. Jones has cynically said that you cannot trust trustees.' Or, again, 'The cynic who is perpetually lowering our confidence in ourselves.' Now all this is not to be cynical; all this is not the action of the cynic; it is the action, perhaps, exaggerated, but clearly intense, of a man complaining of evil; of a man inflamed with anger at the power of evil. Whereas a cynic is a man accepting evil with a smile.

No harm would be done if the word had been frankly transposed (as many words have been) to a new meaning, and if some new word had arisen expressing the reality which was formerly expressed by the word 'cynic' in its original sense. But no such word is proposed, nor has any arisen. What has happened has been a breakdown in that instrument of thought necessary to society called human speech.

The word 'cad' sprang, I believe, originally from the French word 'cadet,' the younger son. It spread out into a lot of meanings—certain forms of service particularly; while the old word 'cadet' went on meaning what it had originally meant, a young fellow engaged in the beginnings of a career. And so on. Meanwhile, 'cad' had taken on a perfectly definite and valuable meaning, signifying a male who lacked certain moral characters attached to the word 'gentleman.' In this transformation no harm was done. We still have the word for expressing a younger son, and we have a word 'cad,' which means something totally different; it being patent to all eyes that many elder sons are cads. But in the case of the word 'cynic,' this process has not taken place. The old word has been given a false meaning, and no new word has arisen nor any old form been preserved to express what 'cynic' used to mean.

Or consider the word 'patriotism.' That ought to be simple enough. A 'patriot' was a man who loved his country. It is rapidly coming to mean a man who will always praise whatever is being done in his country, who is too stupid or too ignorant or too frightened to criticise what has been done badly in his own country. Through the false use of this word, there has arisen a habit of false criticism. If an Englishman travelling abroad says that this or that in England is badly done, he is 'unpatriotic.' If at home he attempts to correct an abuse, he is 'unpatriotic.' If he talks the most dangerous nonsense in mere acceptance of an ill custom grown general he is 'patriotic.' Here is a case of a false word actually corrupting morals and endangering the State.

Or take the word 'sentimental.' Here you have another form of abuse; bad ambiguity. Not ambiguity through the impossibility of defining a powerful but undefinable emotion, but ambiguity through sloppiness. One man objects to an innocent man being hanged; he is 'sentimental.' Another man refuses to make a profit because it involves the sacrifice of something of which he is fond. Another man prefers his ancestral home to a better built or even more hideous house, or his father's and grandfather's furniture to a hotel. He also is 'sentimental.'

Now the word 'sentimental' did once connote something worth remarking, to wit, the tendency of men to have their cake and eat it too. It cannot mean both that and at the same time a susceptibility to the emotion of justice, a susceptibility to the emotion of beauty, a susceptibility to the emotion of familiar affection. When we say, 'for sentimental reasons, William refused to prosecute his aged mother for debts owed to him,' we do not mean the same thing as we mean when we say 'the general sacrificed victory to a sentimental feeling in favour of ancient buildings which he would not destroy for the purpose of military success.' Here, again, if we had a new word to substitute for the old one, if we had a new word which meant for everybody 'sacrificing the greater to the less through emotional weakness' or 'a shutting our eyes to the reality in

269

order to feel more comfortable,' then the degradation of the word would do no harm; but as things are now it does great harm. Many a man is afraid of expressing honest emotion because the word 'sentimental' frightens him. This trait does most harm of all in the department of justice. For the emotion of justice itself is coming to be called 'sentimental.'

Well, then, let us set all this right. But it cannot be done.

XXXII

On Not Knowing Where One Is Going

THE OTHER DAY I WAS GOING THROUGH THE MUNIMENT ROOM OF A GREAT HOUSE, WHICH had behind it rather over two hundred and fifty years of history; and I there discovered one more example of a thing I had found over and over again, which is, that men reach the higher or lower places to which they attain (above or below their ambition) without intention and upon the drift of a tide. No doubt the man who exercises judgment and will in critical turnings goes further (upwards or *downwards*) than the man who does not. He will have a longer run of good or evil fortune than a less skilful or a less determined one; but he knows no more than the weakest what he is to arrive at.

Oliver Cromwell said it in one of those very rare outbreaks of truth from his lips, for as a rule Oliver Cromwell feared the truth with a natural dread. But as he was also a very nervous, impulsive man, it broke out from him willy-nilly at times, and one

271

of these times was that in which he said: 'A man never goes so far as when he does not know where he is going.'

That, indeed, was what the French call 'A cry from the heart!' Here was a bewildered man, finding himself suddenly in exceptional power, and wondering how he got there.

I have heard the same thing all my life long; from poets who wondered to find themselves ignored; from men who commanded a winning battle, and men who commanded a losing one; from those who had made money (which is the modern idea of greatness) and from those who had lost it.

It is true that those who have made money are soon convinced by flatterers, and by their own silly pride, that they willed it all from the beginning. At least, they are so convinced on the surface. But within their hearts they know very well that the thing was a glorious accident, and they inwardly and secretly marvel how it can have come about. You may prove the truth of this in two excellent ways. One is the terror these men are in of new investments, and the other is the rapidity with which they often lose the money they have made.

The man who loses a fortune is of exactly the same stamp as the man who makes one (I know that this sounds like blasphemy in the ears of the suddenly rich, but it is true); he also had no idea where he was going, till he landed up in the gutter. But just as the oddly enriched man is tempted to put down his accident to character, so is the oddly impoverished man. He will recite till you weary the sufferings he has undergone from the nobility of his temper, and perhaps the details of a dreadful boycott which has been plotted against him.

Yet both these men with different fortunes have only followed the common path of accident. Neither of them knew in the least where he was going as he drifted along.

Do you suppose that Napoleon, when he jumped for joy to get that first command of an army in Italy, foresaw the astonishing ten years before him? Or that Alexander, fussing on this side of Asia before Arbela, foresaw the thinness of that eggshell which he cracked? (yet he was born to a kingdom). Do you suppose that any one of the great poets, even if he lived to die full of praise, foresaw in youth the permanent place he would hold in the story of Europe? Do you suppose that any one of the three hundred and twenty-five geniuses who are filling our decade, foresees the complete and miserable oblivion into which he shall have fallen by 1955?

It is a great argument for hereditary government that greatness, under this form of society, is a mere label that tempts men to no illusions upon their personal value. A duke is a duke because his father or second-cousin-twice-removed was a duke. He does not say to himself: 'Here I am, the great Duke; and I made myself what I am.' And a king is a king in the same way. He would be clearly a fool if he boasted of his position as something acquired, though he may rightfully boast of qualities which he possesses as a man. If he is strong or skilful at a game, he would be a hypocrite to deny it; but he is not a king through any powers of his own. To have society ordered in this fashion would, therefore, seem to make for reality; for the avoidance of illusion, and of that horrible falsehood called pride.

We none of us know where we are going. I have seen placards in the street of late, put up by sundry rich men (men suddenly rich) who own newspapers. They ask the passer-by, 'Is there a Hell?' Were I myself one of these suddenly enriched men I would have been a little more reticent. I would not have asked the world to answer such a question. I can tell them this much, that when they are dead they will be in a bad way; though in what degree of a bad way none can tell. But, anyhow, by asking this question (which they bawl at the top of their voices over all London) they are at least admitting that in the most important matter of all they do not quite know where they are going; and I agree.

It reminds me of the excellent three lines upon the two politicians:

> Lump says that Caliban's of gutter breed;
> And Caliban says Lump's a fool indeed;
> And Caliban and Lump and I are all agreed.

No man knows where he is going. It is but the other day that a lot of honest people, most of them frightfully poor, a dozen or so comfortably off, and perhaps a couple of them really well-to-do, got into a train which they confidently believed would land them, if I remember right, at Dorking. But the train took them all imaginable ways, through the east of Surrey and a little bit of Kent, and triumphantly landed them back again in London, having given them a run for their money far longer than that for which they had paid. It is but just to the Company to say that it did not charge them for the extra mileage.

There was a man who went out to look for donkeys

275

and found a kingdom—which is much the same thing. There was another man who set out to do very hard work in order to maintain his family, pursued this course for over fifty years, and was astonished to discover that he had reached Paradise —but only after a certain shock called Death. There are men who write what they know perfectly well to be abominably bad popular verse. They hear it repeated and re-repeated. The more intelligent of them are ashamed of their crapulous lack of art; yet they cannot but be pleased with the praise they receive. They did not know where they were going. There are even men who fall in love at twenty-one, and die abandoned at sixty, in garrets, desperate; so transformed is early glory. What is really more remarkable, my little companions, is this: there are men who marry for money or convenience and discover themselves to have met the fairy *Mélisande*.

The whole world, then, is at cross-purposes. My blessing on it for being so. It would, indeed, be a more abominable place than it is (if that were possible) were all subject to our calculation, and did we know where we are going—which none of us do. I had a friend, a most intimate friend, who told me in early life that it was a good tip to expect the worst, for thus one would receive no disappointment.

I did not follow his advice; but I watched him living by that same doctrine, and I discovered him to be at last abominably disappointed.

Again, the other day a man who had become the head of a very important business (this is true and I know he will forgive me if he reads these lines) told me that, while all envied him, he himself felt his life to be a failure. Whom I answered in my profound wisdom: 'We all feel that, except the men who have been incapable of desiring the things beyond this world.' To which he replied: 'Yes, yes; no doubt, no doubt.'

And that reminds me about a story of a Banker who became a Monk—but I must now end.

XXXIII

The Creative Muse

MY CONTEMPORARIES ARE ALWAYS PROPHESYING WHAT WILL HAPPEN IF SUCH and such a new development comes to pass, and their prophecies are always wrong.

I wonder that they have never tackled the, to me, really interesting problem of what would happen with the spread of gratuitous, cheerful and complete mendacity. There is no reason why we should not get it. It is difficult or impossible to punish—so long as the perpetrator keeps off money—and it is at anyone's hand.

Very few people in any generation have indulged in it, but what would happen if it spread?

That has never been discussed. All vices are spreading. Most of them rapidly. This one, being comparatively innocent, has not yet made a start; but I live in hopes.

We are all designed by a mysterious but beneficent Providence to expect the statements of our fellow-beings to be false; but false with a purpose; usually with the purpose of becoming richer at our expense—often with the purpose of getting out of doing us some service; oftener with the purpose of magnifying the speaker, as, by boasting acquaintance with any lord, or by casual allusion to his own lineage. But we have no safeguard against beatific mendacity, mendacity 'joyous, fresh and clear,' to use the adjectives applied by a famous Prussian to the Great War—before he had enjoyed it.

There have always been a few people to practise this art, and it is one of the most captivating extravagances of innocent childhood, but I am supposing its general spread among men and women, and wondering how we should deal with it.

For instance, you go into a country inn near a railway station and you say, 'Can you tell me when the next train goes to London?' The innkeeper answers, looking at his watch, 'One of the best trains of the day has just gone, but if you care to take a short walk and come back at five minutes to six you will be in time to take the six two, which gets to Waterloo without stopping anywhere, except at Basingstoke. There is a "third" Pullman on board and they serve a meal, if you want it.' You say, 'Thank you,' drink some chemical waters for the good of the house (if it is within the hours allowed by the millionaires) and take your stroll, admiring, perhaps, the distant view. You return at five minutes to six to discover that the last train for London—until a very slow one near midnight—left ten minutes before. The barmaid tells you that her master is out, and is not coming back that evening, so you cannot even have your revenge.

I met a man of this sort once in the Welsh hills. He could not talk much English, for he was a poor man, but the little English that he could talk was very much to the purpose, as you shall hear.

It was on the northern side of Plynlimmon, getting down to the marshy flat that is there, where also are, or were in those days, certain habitations of men. It was getting dark. I was exceedingly tired and I had come a very long way, climbing over the big hill; and I asked a man whom I saw approaching me whether it were far to Machynlleth. He told me circumstantially and in a charming accent that it was more than a quarter of an hour away— maybe twenty minutes—'going as you are going.' He then gave me a list of the inns in Machynlleth, expatiating upon each its advantages and disadvantages. He told me the name of a friend of his who kept one inn in particular (which he recommended), and he said if I were to mention his name (which he gave me) I should receive an especial welcome. He then told me a lot about his friend, and how his wife was an Englishwoman, but disfigured by the loss of one eye. I thanked him warmly, for he had really taken trouble, and I went on across the moor.

As soon as it was dark I was already on a track which I guessed would end in a proper road, and I went on and on and on, I cannot tell you how long. There was no moon, nor even stars. It was a pitch-black night and cold. Then it began to rain. Still I saw no sign of Machynlleth. When I got there at last I was at the far end of endeavour, but just alive enough to be very angry indeed with the Cymric One who had thus indulged in the great human creative faculty—that noble power wherein we resemble the gods—by telling me it was only a quarter of an hour away.

Now, when I got into Machynlleth, the first thing I saw was a policeman, whom I asked at once for the hotel the man had told me of—so strong, in spite of deception, is our faith in our fellow-beings. The policeman told me that there was no such hotel, let alone any such hotelkeeper, as I had been told of. He knew them all. Not one had a wife with one eye. After thinking it out carefully he advised me to go to a particular house, which was designed, as I discovered, neither for the rich nor for the poor. Upon the whole it was more suitable for the poor. There I looked up a directory to confirm not my faith, but my anger, and sure enough the policeman at least was telling the truth. The hotel which the man on the mountain-side had given me was—like great Achilles, or the lively nymph sweet Echo—a phantasm; a thing of man's mind.

Now, I can excuse this lying man upon one plea only: that he may have been a Fairy. Once you get through the Marches of Wales you may like as not come across such beings, and when you are past Llanidloes the hills are full of them. If he was a human being I am angry with him to this day.

But the thing is still rare. What would happen if it spread? Think how all day long you are trusting what your fellow-beings say; at least, in the rough, and when they have no apparent reason for lying. Think of what would happen to your day if they were always romancing at large, only for fun, and embroidering with circumstantial detail the lies they chose to tell.

Supposing the ordinary gambit, instead of being about the weather, were a spontaneous and merry lie. Supposing, for instance, a shopman in Balham were to tell you of a morning, in a nice, happy, human way, that it was well worth going into town to see the charred remains of the Albert Hall, which had been burned down in the small hours, too late for the newspapers to print the news. Or supposing, as you got into your office, a man passing by were to stop and tell you that it was most urgent for you to take a taxicab at once for some very distant address he should give you and that he had been specially asked to give you the message as he was going your way, naming great business awaiting you. Or supposing one's host, when one came down to breakfast in another man's house, were to suggest an interesting motor drive, making everything ready for it, and then go out on his own and leave you to do the same; there being no motor and no such place as that of which he had given you a careful description. What then?

It is no good telling me that we already have a foretaste of this state of affairs in reading the daily papers. That is not the same thing. The daily papers do not indulge their fictions upon matters which have no relation at all to reality; or, at least, when they do, it is not the kind of thing that immediately affects our daily lives. They may expatiate upon the beauty and eloquence of some politician who looks and talks like an animal, but they do not tell you that there will be a royal procession down Pall Mall on a day when nothing of the sort is being thought of. In fact, I cannot help thinking it is rather a pity they don't. It would be a livelier form of (what shall I call it? Equivocation?) than they habitually indulge in.

Before I end all this nonsense, let me tell you a true story. Not that the other was not true, but this is especially and particularly true, being quite fresh in my mind from only the other day.

I had occasion to cross the Channel in a large liner—not one of the ordinary boats. As the ship I was on had not started by the time she was advertised to start I asked a selection of officials when she would start, and when she would get in, and when we should be allowed to get off and land. They all gave me different answers: the answers differing by as much as three hours between the extremes (although the total distance could have been covered in that time). But there was one man—a young sailor—who was at the pains of giving me a most detailed account, telling me exactly why we were delayed, how the obstacle was being got rid of, almost to a minute when we were to start, what would happen on the way, the sort of weather we should have, when we should pass the breakwater of the further harbour, how long we should be kept on board before being allowed to land—and so on. I listened to him fascinated, for I had met this type before, and knew them to be the sons of the Muses, followers of far-darting Apollo, but no good at anything else. Naturally I did not believe a word he said; and he alone, as it turned out, had told me the truth and the exact truth in every detail. The moral of that, as of everything else, is that you never can tell.

XXXIV

A Remaining Christmas

THE WORLD IS CHANGING VERY FAST, AND NEITHER EXACTLY FOR THE BETTER NOR FOP the worse, but for division. Our civilisation is splitting more and more into two camps, and what was common to the whole of it is becoming restricted to the Christian, and soon will be restricted to the Catholic half.

That is why I have called this article 'A Remaining Christmas.' People ask themselves how much remains of this observance and of the feast and its customs. Now a concrete instance is more vivid and, in its own way, of more value than a general appreciation. So I will set down here exactly what Christmas still is in a certain house in England, how it is observed, and all the domestic rites accompanying it in their detail and warmth.

This house stands low down upon clay near a little river. It is quite cut off from the towns; no one has built near it. Every cottage for a mile and more is old, with here and there a modern addition. The church of the parish (which was lost of course three and a half centuries ago, under Elizabeth) is as old as the Crusades. It is of the twelfth century. The house of which I speak is in its oldest parts of the fourteenth century at least, and perhaps earlier, but there are modern additions. One wing of it was built seventy years ago at the south end of the house, another at the north end, twenty years ago. Yet the tradition is so strong that you would not tell from the outside, and hardly from the inside, which part is old and which part is new. For, indeed, the old part itself grew up gradually, and the eleven gables of the house show up against the sky as though they were of one age, though in truth they are of every age down along all these five hundred years and more.

The central upper room of the house is the chapel where Mass is said, and there one sees, uncovered by any wall of plaster or brick, the original structure of the house, which is of vast oaken beams, the main supports and transverse pieces half a yard across, mortised strongly into each other, and smoothed roughly with the adze. They are black with the years. The roof soars up like a high-pitched tent, and is supported by a whole fan of lesser curved oaken beams. There is but one window behind the altar. Indeed, the whole house is thus in its structure of the local and native oak and the brick walls of it are only curtains built in between the wooden framework of that most ancient habitation.

Beneath the chapel is the dining-room, where there is a very large open hearth which can take huge logs and which is as old as anything in the place. Here wood only is burnt, and that wood oak.

Down this room there runs a very long oaken table as dark with age almost as the beams above it, and this table has a history. It came out of one of the Oxford colleges when the Puritans looted them three hundred years ago. It never got back to its original home. It passed from one family to another until at last it was purchased (in his youth and upon his marriage) by the man who now owns this house. Those who know about such things give its date as the beginning of the seventeenth century. It was made, then, while Shakespeare was still living, and while the faith of England still hung in the balance; for one cannot say that England was certain to lose her Catholicism finally till the first quarter of that century was passed. This table, roughly carved at the side, has been polished with wax since first it began to bear food for men, and now the surface shines like a slightly, very slightly, undulating sea in a calm. At night the brass candle-sticks (for this house is lit with candles, as the proper light for men's eyes) are reflected in it as in still brown water; so are the vessels of glass and of silver and of pewter, and the flagons of wine. No cloth is ever spread to hide this venerable splendour, nor, let us hope, ever will be.

At one end of the house, where the largest of its many outer doors (there are several such) swings massively upon huge forged iron hinges, there is a hall, not very wide, its length as great as the width of the house and its height very great for its width. Like the chapel, its roof soars up, steep and dark, so that from its floor (which is made of very great and heavy slabs of the local stone) one looks up to the roof-tree itself. This hall has another great wide hearth in it for the burning of oak, and there is an oaken staircase, very wide and of an easy slope, with an oaken balustrade and leading up to an open gallery above, whence you look down upon the place. Above this gallery is a statue of Our Lady, carved in wood, uncoloured, and holding the Holy Child, and beneath her many shelves of books. This room is panelled, as are so many of the rooms of the house, but it has older panels than any of the others, and the great door of it opens on to the high road.

Now the way Christmas is kept in this house is this:

On Christmas Eve a great quantity of holly and of laurel is brought in from the garden and from the farm (for this house has a farm of 100 acres attached to it and an oak wood of ten acres). This greenery is put all over the house in every room just before it becomes dark on that day. Then there is brought into the hall a young pine tree, about twice the height of a man, to serve for a Christmas tree, and on this innumerable little candles are fixed, and presents for all the household and the guests and the children of the village.

It is at about five o'clock that these last come into the house, and at that hour in England, at that date, it has long been quite dark; so they come into a house all illuminated, with the Christmas tree shining like a cluster of many stars seen through a glass.

The first thing after the entry of these people from the village and their children (the children are in number about fifty—for this remote place keeps a good level through the generations and does not shrink or grow, but remains itself) is a common meal, where all eat and drink their fill in the offices. Then the children come in to the Christmas tree. They are each given a silver piece one by one, and one by one their presents. After that they dance in the hall and sing songs, which have been handed down to them for I do not know how long. These songs are game-songs, and are sung to keep time with the various parts in each game, and the men and things and animals which you hear mentioned in these songs are all of that country-side. Indeed, the tradition of Christmas here is what it should be everywhere, knit into the very stuff of the place; so that I fancy the little children, when they think of Bethlehem, see it in their minds as though it were in the winter depth of England, which is as it should be.

These games and songs continue for as long as they will, and then they file out past the great fire in the hearth to a small place adjoining where a crib has been set up with images of Our Lady and St. Joseph and the Holy Child, the Shepherds, and what I will call, by your leave, the Holy Animals. And here, again, tradition is so strong in this house that these figures are never new-bought, but are as old as the oldest of the children of the family, now with children of their own. On this account, the donkey has lost one of its plaster ears, and the old ox which used to be all brown is now piebald, and of the shepherds, one actually has no head. But all that is lacking is imagined. There hangs from the roof of the crib over the Holy Child a tinsel star grown rather obscure after all these years, and much too large for the place. Before this crib the children (some of them Catholic and some Protestant, for the village is mixed) sing their carols; the one they know best is the one which begins, 'The First Good Joy that Mary had, it was the joy of One.' There are half a dozen or so of these carols which the children here sing; and mixed with their voices is the voice of the miller (for this house has a great windmill attached to it). The miller is famous in these parts for his singing, having a very deep and loud voice which is his pride. When these carols are over, all disperse, except those who are living in the house, but the older ones are not allowed to go without more good drink for their viaticum, a sustenance for Christian men.

Then the people of the house, when they have dined, and their guests, with the priest who is to say Mass for them, sit up till near midnight. There is brought in a very large log of oak (you must be getting tired of oak by this time! But everything here is oaken, for the house is of the Weald). This log of oak is the Christmas or Yule log and the rule is that it must be too heavy for one man to lift; so two men come, bringing it in from outside, the master of the house and his servant. They cast it down upon the fire in the great hearth of the dining-room, and the superstition is that, if it burns all night and is found still smouldering in the morning, the home will be prosperous for the coming year.

With that they all go up to the chapel and there the three night Masses are said, one after the other, and those of the household take their Communion.

Next morning they sleep late, and the great Christmas dinner is at midday. It is a turkey, and a plum pudding with holly in it, and everything conventional, and therefore satisfactory, is done. Crackers are pulled, the brandy is lit and poured over the pudding till the holly crackles in the flame and the curtains are drawn a moment that the flames may be seen. This Christmas feast, so great that it may be said almost to fill the day, they may reprove who will; but for my part I applaud.

Now, you must not think that Christmas being over, the season and its glories are at an end, for in this house there is kept up the full custom of the Twelve Days, so that 'Twelfth Day,' the Epiphany, still has, to its inhabitants, its full and ancient meaning as it had when Shakespeare wrote. The green

293

is kept in its place in every room, and not a leaf of it must be moved until Epiphany morning, but on the other hand not a leaf of it must remain in the house, nor the Christmas tree either, by Epiphany evening. It is all taken out and burnt in a special little coppice reserved for these good trees which have done their Christmas duty; and now, after so many years, you might almost call it a little forest, for each tree has lived, bearing witness to the holy vitality of unbroken ritual and inherited things.

In the midst of this season between Christmas and Twelfth Day comes the ceremony of the New Year, and this is how it is observed:

On New Year's Eve, at about a quarter to twelve o'clock at night, the master of the house and all that are with him go about from room to room opening every door and window, however cold the weather be, for thus, they say, the old year and its burdens can go out and leave everything new for hope and for the youth of the coming time.

This also is a superstition, and of the best. Those who observe it trust that it is as old as Europe, and with roots stretching back into forgotten times.

While this is going on the bells in the Church hard by are ringing out the old year, and when all the windows and doors have thus been opened and

294

left wide, all those in the house go outside, listening for the cessation of the chimes, which comes just before the turn of the year. There is an odd silence of a few minutes, and watches are consulted to make certain of the time (for this house detests wireless and has not even a telephone), and the way they know the moment of midnight is by the boom of a gun, which is fired at a town far off, but can always be heard.

At that sound the bells of the church clash out suddenly in new chords, the master of the house goes back into it with a piece of stone or earth from outside, all doors are shut, and the household, all of them, rich and poor, drink a glass of wine together to salute the New Year.

This, which I have just described, is not in a novel or in a play. It is real, and goes on as the ordinary habit of living men and women. I fear that set down thus in our terribly changing time it must sound very strange and, perhaps in places, grotesque, but to those who practise it, it is not only sacred, but normal, having in the whole of the complicated affair a sacramental quality and an effect of benediction: not to be despised.

Indeed, modern men, who lack such things, lack

sustenance, and our fathers who founded all those ritual observances were very wise.

*   *   *   *   *

Man has a body as well as a soul, and the whole of man, soul and body, is nourished sanely by a multiplicity of observed traditional things. Moreover, there is this great quality in the unchanging practice of Holy Seasons, that it makes explicable, tolerable and normal what is otherwise a shocking and intolerable and, even in the fullest sense, abnormal thing. I mean, the mortality of immortal man.

Not only death (which shakes and rends all that is human in us, creating a monstrous separation and threatening the soul with isolation which destroys) not only death, but that accompaniment of mortality which is a perpetual series of lesser deaths and is called change, is challenged, chained, and put in its place by unaltered and successive acts of seasonable regard for loss and dereliction and mutability. The threats of despair, remorse, necessary expiation, weariness almost beyond bearing, dull repetition of things apparently fruitless, unnecessary and without meaning, estrangement, the misunderstanding of mind by mind, forgetfulness which is a false alarm, grief and repentance, which are true ones, but of a sad company, young men perished in battle before their parents had lost vigour in age, the perils of sickness in the body and even in the mind, anxiety, honour harassed, all the bitterness of living—become part of a large business which may lead to Beatitude. For they are all connected in the memory with holy day after holy day, year by year, binding the generations together; carrying on even in this world, as it were, the life of the dead and giving corporate substance, permanence and stability, without the symbol of which (at least) the vast increasing burden of life might at last conquer us and be no longer borne.

This house where such good things are done year by year has suffered all the things that every age has suffered. It has known the sudden separation of wife and husband, the sudden fall of young men under arms who will never more come home, the scattering of the living and their precarious return, the increase and the loss of fortune, all those terrors and all those lessenings and haltings and failures of hope which make up the life of man. But its Christmas binds it to its own past and promises its future; making the house an undying thing of which those subject to mortality within it are members, sharing in its continuous survival.

It is not wonderful that of such a house verse should be written. Many verses have been so written commemorating and praising this house. The last verse written of it I may quote here by way of ending:

'Stand thou for ever among human Houses,
    House of the Resurrection, House of Birth;
House of the rooted hearts and long carouses,
    Stand, and be famous over all the Earth.'